TAKE A STAND

FOR YOUR BRAND

BUILDING A GREAT AGENCY BRAND FROM THE INSIDE OUT

Tim Williams

For further information, contact:
The Copy Workshop
2144 N. Hudson • Chicago, IL 60614
(773) 871-1179 • Fax: (773) 281-4643
www.adbuzz.com or thecopyworkshop@aol.com

Contents

SECTION 5 *The Outcome Of Building An Agency Brand*

APPENDIX

FOREWORD:
The Fine Art of Herding Cats

This book is written primarily for owners and managers of advertising agencies, public relations firms, design firms, interactive firms, sales promotion firms, brand consultancies, media buying services, and other kinds of marketing communications companies.

Without question, the practices in this book can be applied to other kinds of organizations as well. That's because this isn't about the latest management fads, but rather about how companies can define themselves as brands, and how they can bring that brand to life in every part of their organization.

But this book focuses on advertising agencies because agencies are my area of expertise. I've spent the better part of three decades in the agency business, working my way up through the ranks of Madison Avenue, founding my own firm, managing a top-100 agency, then applying my experience as a consultant to agencies throughout the U.S. and abroad.

Advertising agencies are also among the toughest companies to manage. If you can learn to successfully lead and manage an advertising agency (which is not unlike herding cats), you can certainly do the same with a gentler, saner kind of company.

As I've worked with agencies throughout the years, I've observed how engaging in transformational work can be one of the most satisfying experiences of an agency executive's career. If nothing else, in the daily tedium of business life, it helps you realize that you really *can* make a difference. Your agency *can* change. And you *can* enjoy your job again, just like you did when you first got into the business.

While this book advances several new perspectives on the agency business, you'll also find that many of the concepts are more foundational than revolutionary. But like great sports teams, it's the fundamentals that make great agencies. And sometime that in and of itself is a revolutionary thought. Because as the years roll by, agency managers can easily get caught up in the "thick of thin things." We get distracted and forget that the agencies we truly admire got that way by being brilliant on the basics.

Make no mistake, making the decision to adopt a differentiating business strategy is very, very difficult for advertising agencies, most of whom desperately want to be all things to all people. And once that all-important decision has been made, the work of building the agency brand from the inside out amounts to a lot of personal commitment, follow up, and just plain hard work.

I mean this book to be a wake-up call and a challenge to introspection. There's a big difference between knowing and doing — hence the use of examples, sidebars, checklists, and the chapters at the end of the book on the subject of performance.

I promise that if you'll engage yourself, be willing to re-consider things you know but don't do, and lead by example, you and everyone around you will find new meaning in your work. I've seen this transformation at agencies large and small. As an agency owner or manager, building your agency brand is your most important job and offers the most enjoyment you can have in your career.

THE AGENCY AS A BRAND

1 THE AGENCY AS A BRAND: Doing For Yourself What You Do For Your Clients

ADVERTISING AGENCIES, LIKE EVERYTHING ELSE, ARE BRANDS. Yet as a group, agencies are as undifferentiated as cows on a hillside. Of the 12,000 firms in America that call themselves "advertising agencies," painfully few of them have a unique reputation of any kind. When you deal with clients in this situation, chances are you would help them carve out a meaningful position in the marketplace. You would help them develop a branding strategy.

Agencies need to do for themselves what they do for their clients: build a strong, distinctive, memorable brand. But they are usually so eager to be a "full-service integrated agency" that they try to stand for everything. Crack the pages of a typical agency brochure and you see language like this:

> "Jones & Smith is a full-service, diversified marketing communications firm serving a wide variety of client, from health care to high technology. From advertising to public relations, from television to Web sites, we offer comprehensive solutions to every client's marketing problems."

Or this:

> "The Roberts Group is dedicated to making clients successful by generating results through effective advertising, public relations, and related marketing communications."

Agencies need to do for themselves what they do for their clients: build a strong brand.

While it's good and noble to want to produce results for a client, that should be the purpose of *every* agency. There's nothing differentiating about the notion of producing results. There's also nothing differentiating about being "full-service," "diversified," "integrated," or "comprehensive."

Is it any wonder that most clients have no idea what distinguishes one agency from another? Standing for everything is just another way of standing for nothing. As Bill Bernbach said, "If you stand for something, you will always find some people for you and some against you. If you stand for nothing, you will find nobody against you, and nobody *for* you."[1]

Another way of looking at the issue of branding for agencies is to ask, "What reason can we give prospective clients outside our market to do business with us?" Most agency-client relationships are the result of proximity – you simply happen to be close by. But what about the larger accounts (with more money) that are 2,000 miles away? How can you throw your hat into *that* ring?

Allen Rosenshine, former CEO of BBDO, observed, "Over the last decade, agency identities have become more muddled, less distinguished, and unfortunately, more like commodities than brands. And every day we come dangerously closer to confusing our clients about who we are, what we are, and why we are valuable to their business."[2]

Imagine the credibility problem of a restaurant claiming to specialize in French and Mexican and Brazilian food. Ad agencies are no different. An agency that puts everything on its menu might as well have no menu at all. As Confucius said, "Man who chases two rabbits catches neither."

Standing for everything is just another way of standing for nothing.

Brand strategist Adam Morgan wisely observes that when it comes to defining a brand, we must not only decide what we are, but what we are *not*.[3] It jolts many agency professionals to realize that the goal of defining a strong agency brand isn't to try to appeal to a larger number of clients, but fewer. A great Thai restaurant appeals only to those who like Thai cuisine, not everybody who likes food.

A BRAND IS MORE THAN A FAMILIAR NAME

Just because others have heard of your agency doesn't mean you have an agency brand. Name awareness and brand equity are only indirectly related. A lot of us have heard of agency names but we have no idea who they are, what they do, or what they stand for. These agencies have name awareness but no brand equity.

Branding puts meat on the bones of simple awareness. Once a prospective client knows the answer to the question, "Who are those guys?" the next question he has is "What are these guys all about?"

Just like any other product category, clients like to buy brands, not generic products.

THE GENERALIST VS. THE SPECIALIST

"If the essence of advertising is differentiation," observes one agency executive, "not only are all agency offerings virtually indistinguishable, so is the level of differentiation that they can offer their clients. There are now hundreds of virtually identical agencies, all producing an un-original me-too product."[4]

It's a challenge to distinguish one firm from another in a world of agency generalists. Consider what a difference it would make if your agency became more of a specialist. For starters, who charges more for their services, the generalist or the specialist? A family doctor or a brain surgeon? Not only does the specialist make more money, but a good brain surgeon is likely to attract business from all over the country, not just his own community. And brain surgeons don't compete with every other doctor in the country – only other brain surgeons. Could this logic possibly apply to ad agencies?

Marketing consultant Jack Trout argues that being a specialist creates a strong halo effect:

> "People are impressed with those who concentrate on a specific activity or product. They perceive them as experts…Conversely, the generalist is rarely given expertise in many fields of endeavor no matter how good he or she may be. Common sense tells the prospect that a single person or company cannot be expert in everything."[5]

Why have traditional department stores died while niche players like Home Depot, PetsMart, and Office Max have thrived? It's a story of the generalist vs. the specialist.

Business consultants Michael Treacy and Fred Wiersema advise companies to stop trying to be all things to all people and instead find the unique value that it alone can deliver to a chosen market. The essence of their best-selling book, *The Discipline of Market Leaders*, can be distilled into three sentences. "Choose your customers. Narrow your focus. Dominate your market." [6]

It's just like the client who wants everything in his ad to be of equal size – the photo, the headline, the copy, the logo. Wise agencies remind their clients that all emphasis is no emphasis. The same is true for the way agencies position themselves.

YOU CAN'T PLEASE ALL OF THE PEOPLE ALL OF THE TIME

Agencies do a great job of helping their clients achieve distinction in the marketplace. There's no reason why your agency can't do the same – with a distinctive philosophy, distinctive capabilities, a distinctive identity, and a distinctive way of doing business.

In other words, you shouldn't just be concerned with building an agency, but with building an agency *brand*. Jim Mullen, founder of the respected Mullen agency says, "A smart organization takes pains to define its brand identity and manage its public perceptions among all of its key constituencies by continuously reinforcing its core values. Only a foolish organization will allow its brand perceptions to be shaped by the street or, worse yet, by its competitors." [7] Yet, more often than not, that's how most agency reputations are created.

If you transform your agency from a commodity into a brand, you will naturally exclude some people. Not everybody will be a prospective client. That's because branding means creating strong, sometime polarizing differences. Some clients will be attracted to you and some won't. That's O.K., because the ones who are attracted are *strongly* attracted. And that's what gives the agency its competitive advantage.

It's a scary proposition for most firms to think about intentionally limiting their audience.

But, as Bill Cosby once said, "I can't give you the formula for success, but I can give you the formula for failure: try and please everybody."

UNDERPROMISING AND OVERDELIVERING

You could visit, at random, any one of the thousands of companies who call themselves advertising agencies (or design firms, or PR firms, brand consultancies), pick up their promotional literature, and you might be tempted to believe that they are very close to perfect.

According to their brochure, they have a reputation for outstanding service, brilliant creative work, attention to detail, making deadlines, delivering out-of-the-box thinking, executing killer media buys, and saving the client money. Not only are claims like these naïve, they are quite unbelievable. Every client knows that very few agencies can do all of that, all of the time.

Ironically, the agencies who really *are* that good never claim to be. They prefer soft sell over hard sell, knowing that the credibility of their brand is at stake. They actually underpromise, then overdeliver. They usually produce not just better work than other agencies, but *vastly* better work. In fact, on every important dimension of quality, great agency brands are a clear cut above the norm.

Defining your agency brand means not only deciding what you are, but what you are not.

A strong agency brand is a brand with both substance and style. The substance part is unequivocally first and foremost. I can't count the number of times I've walked into the lobby of what looks like a very impressive agency (a lot of style) only to find that behind the marble reception desk lies an agency that's no better than any other (very little substance).

A fashionable look is not a brand. A cool business card is not a brand. A staff that dresses entirely in black is not a brand. These could all be *elements* of an agency brand, but not the *essence*. The best agency brands don't just have quality offices, they have quality work. And they don't just talk about producing quality work – they actually do it.

DISCOVERING YOUR AGENCY BRAND

You don't define your agency brand as much as you *discover* it. It's already there, deep inside your agency soul, in the form of your natural strengths and core competencies. When you plumb the depths of your agency character, you begin to wonder about several crucial questions:

- What is the best way to focus our agency for the future?
- What do we need to change to achieve our new focus?
- How can we make sure we stay true to our new focus for the long term?

The key word here is focus – the willingness to stand for something.

Discovering the agency brand cannot be a matter of deciding the future of the agency over lunch. To produce a lasting effect, defining the brand must involve all the major stakeholders: principals, management, and employees. The best place to start is by asking all of these groups their opinions about where the agency is *now*. You can usually get a good read on this by asking five simple (but not easy) questions:

1. Does the agency have a distinctive mission or positioning that makes it different from other agencies? If so, how would you define it?
2. How well do you think the agency lives up to its mission or positioning?
3. Should the agency's mission or positioning be different? If so, how?
4. What do you perceive to be the agency's greatest strength?
5. What do you perceive to be the agency's greatest weakness?

In most agencies, the answer to question number one is usually "no." Comments like these are common:

> "I don't recall ever reading or hearing the mission of the agency. It's not even in the company brochure or in the employee manual."

> "I haven't been aware of an official agency mission other than producing great advertising and making lots of money."

Those willing to take a stab at attempting to describe the "mission" usually do it in vague terms:

"To provide outstanding creative solutions to every advertising, marketing and public relations challenge."

"To offer the best advertising, PR and other marketing communications to our clients."

"To serve all of our clients' communications needs."

It may or may not surprise you to learn that for most agencies, this is as good as it gets. Pretty pathetic for the industry that invented positioning.

As you start out on the journey of developing a brand for your agency, here's a framework that you can follow.

PURPOSE, PRINCIPLES AND POSITIONING

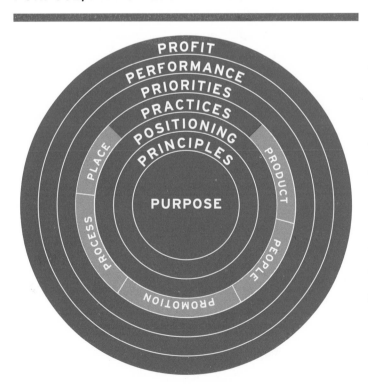

At the foundation of an agency's brand are its purpose, its principles, and its positioning. Over the years, practices may change, but purpose, principles, and positioning remain constant. They are the anchors in the storm of business.

Purpose

The process of branding your agency starts with *purpose* – the agency's reason for being. Some companies think in terms of "mission," or "mission statement."

But "purpose" is a much more defining concept. For one thing, most mission statements are about as useful as the aluminum they're framed in. They hang in the company lobby as proof that management has completed the requisite off-site retreat and can now cross "mission statement" off their list.

Forget about the mission statement and look deeply at the question, "What makes us get out of bed in the morning?" (The answer, by the way, should not be to make more money. Every occupation provides that opportunity.) Why did you choose to spend your lives in the business of advertising, marketing, or public relations? If you don't know – or can't remember – it's *really* time to think about your true purpose.

Principles

Next, think about your *principles*, a set of strongly held values that guide your business decisions. Principles are a slice of the agency's DNA.

In a given business situation, well-defined principles inspire discussion and engender debate. They make you stop and really think about the decisions you're making. Principles help you draw a line in the sand.

Principles give meaning to our otherwise commercial existence. They are like a compass that gives us direction. They show us true north. The litmus test is to ask the question, "Would we stick to these principles no matter what?" If you can answer yes, even when that means a missed financial opportunity, you've found your principles.

Positioning

Ken Roman, the former head of Ogilvy & Mather, was fond of reminding his staff, "The essence of positioning is sacrifice."[8] That's why defining a brand is so difficult for agencies; it involves sacrifice. It means giving something up. It means not only deciding what you are, but what you are not. In fact, sacrifice is the very core of defining a successful agency brand.

As branding consultant Al Ries says, "If there is no sacrifice, there is no branding strategy."[9] In branding your agency, the goal is to be exclusive, not inclusive. To divide perceptions, not unify them. To appeal to some clients, but not all clients.

To most agency principals, this is pretty scary stuff. But ultimately, agencies need to find the answer to the question, what reason can we give important prospective clients outside our city to do business with us? Just like any other successful product or service, agencies need a meaningful and distinctive position in the marketplace.

Practices

Once your positioning has been defined, it's time to ask the soul-searching question, "What needs to change in our organization in order for us to bring our positioning to life in everything we do?"

It's not just a matter of producing a slick new agency brochure, ordering new letter-head, and revising the Web site. Branding starts from the inside out. It's reflected in five important areas of your business (which, coincidently, all start with the letter "P"):

- Your *product*
- Your *people*
- Your *promotion*
- Your *process*
- Your *place* of business

Bringing the agency brand to life is all about aligning your product, people, process, promotion, and place to support the brand. In other words, it's about *aligning your practices with your positioning*. Agencies that are serious about establishing an agency brand begin to ask questions like this:

Product

1. Do we need to add new services and capabilities?
2. Do we have the right clients?
3. Do we need to do a better job of integrating your services and capabilities?
4. Do we need to find new business partners?
5. Do we need to develop new strategic alliances?

People

1. Do we have the right people with the right skills?
2. Do we have them in the right assignments?
3. What kind of new people do we need to hire to support our agency brand?
4. Have we clearly defined roles and responsibilities for all employees?
5. Have we adequately defined our expected performance outcomes?
6. What kind of standards should we apply to selecting new employees?
7. What kind of training program do we need to help employees live the brand?

Promotion

1. What immediate changes do we need to make in our agency corporate identity?
2. How can we more narrowly define the criteria we apply to prospective clients?
3. What should we say differently in our self-promotion materials?
4. How should our new business approach change?
5. How can we better use publicity to tell the story of our agency brand?

Process

1. Does the agency need to be organized differently to better support the agency brand?
2. Do we have agency systems and procedures that run counter to the brand?
3. What changes or improvements should we make to the way jobs are processed through the agency?
4. Have we allocated the right resources to the right clients?
5. Is our workload distributed evenly?
6. What changes should we make to the way our services are priced or the way we are compensated?

Place

1. How can we change our working environment to better reflect our positioning?
2. What do we need to do to our offices to make a different first impression?
3. Are we providing an environment in which our people can do their best work?
4. Do our people have the right resources?
5. How can new or different technology help us achieve our branding strategy?

Right about now you might be thinking that you really don't have time for this. After all, you have a business to run. Clients to serve. Payroll to meet. Too many urgent issues and problems to be spending time thinking about fluffy things like agency branding. You could, of course, simply keep doing what you've been doing. Just remember that the definition of insanity is repeating the same behavior expecting different results. And you're really just talking about saving hours when in fact you may be wasting years.

There is no better use of your time than thinking deeply about how to set your agency apart from the competition. "Differentiate or die" is a warning worth heeding.[10] Defining what makes your organization different, then *making* it different, is the best leadership you could possibly provide your agency.

It's also quite possibly the best way to add value to your agency, whether you plan to sell it some day or not. According to most estimates, the average market value of well-branded companies (including agencies) is about 70 percent greater than the value of their tangible assets.

Chances are your agency is already doing a good job of adding value to your clients' companies. How about taking the time to add some value to your own?

DEFINING THE AGENCY BRAND

What makes you get out of bed in the morning?

2 PURPOSE:
Creating A Company
Of Believers

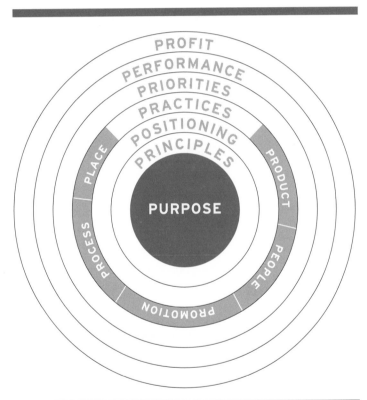

PROFIT IS NOT AT THE center of your business. People are not at the center of your business. Not even the client is at the center of your business. Your *purpose* is – or should be – at the center of your business.

Your purpose is the agency's reason for being. Don't confuse purpose with the typical weak, soggy "mission statements" that hang unnoticed in the lobbies of countless companies across America. Most mission statements are a mélange of hyperbole that is neither unique nor motivating. How motivated would you be by meaningless "mission statements" like these?

"To be an integrated marketing communications firm providing our client's brand with strategic marketing insights, strategic marketing planning and strategic creative solutions."

"To be the agency of choice, recognized as a leader in marketing, driven by creativity, measurable results and community service."

"To help make clients successful by generating results through effective advertising, public relations and related marketing communications."

Is it any wonder why nobody reads or cares about the company mission statement? As adman Joey Reiman says, "Like a tombstone in a cemetery, the mission statement is unveiled, and then we visit it once a year."[1]

Any guesses as to the most commonly used words in mission statements? One analysis puts the words "service, customers, quality, and value," at the top of the list.[2] When words like these get overused in business, they completely lose their meaning. Not to mention the fact that they provide absolutely no point of distinction for a company or an agency.

Consider what your purpose would be if you were creating a movement rather than a business.

What's really needed in place of the tired mission statement is to discover a strong sense of purpose – the thing that makes you and your associates get out of bed in the morning. The notable agencies have an ambitious reason for being. They have a purpose that makes them reach for the stars. Some compare a purpose to a guiding star on the horizon – forever pursued but never reached.[3]

Management expert Peter Drucker believes that a strong sense of purpose gives people a feeling that they are contributing to something greater. Unless we focus our work on making a meaningful contribution, he says, we are not only likely to aim too low, we are likely to aim at the wrong things. All people and all efforts should be focused on contribution – a meaningful end result that will make an important difference for the organization.[4]

Consider that your purpose would be if you were leading a *movement* rather than a business. Movements are about meaning, not commercialism. Movements are about making a difference in the world. They intrinsically motivate people to action. They are filled with a sense of purpose.

"What we need," says the respected management thinker Gary Hamel, "is not an economy of hands or heads, but an economy of hearts. Every employee should feel that he or she is contributing to something that will actually make a genuine and positive difference in the lives of customers and colleagues."[5]

A strong purpose makes the agency feel as if it's engaged in something that's honorable, almost a holy crusade. This creates not just a company of workers, but a company of believers. "The psychology of these high-minded missions is clear," writes Warren Bennis. "People know going in that they will be expected to make sacrifices, but they also know they are doing something monumental, something worthy of their best selves."[6]

The authors of the insightful *Primal Leadership* agree. They observe that knowing your purpose gives leaders the ammunition they need to fight complacency in the organization.

> "Given the primal task of leadership, the ability to inspire and move people with a compelling vision looms large. Inspirational leaders get people excited about a common mission. They offer a sense of purpose beyond the day-to-day tasks or quarterly goals that so often take the place of a meaningful vision. Such leaders know that what people value most deeply will move them most powerfully in their work."[7]

Peters and Waterman, in their early work in the field of excellence, went this far: "We will surrender a great deal to institutions that give us a sense of meaning, and through it, a sense of security."[8] Henry Ford gave us one of the best and earliest examples of corporate purpose when he said, "I will build a motor car for the great multitude. It will be constructed of the best materials, by the best men and women to be hired, after the simplest designs that modern engineering can devise. Any person making a good salary will be able to own one, and enjoy with his family the blessings of hours of pleasure in God's great open spaces."

WHAT DRIVES US FROM INSIDE

Rather than being driven solely by the market, the competition, or the numbers, we have to pay attention to what drives us from inside. Our purpose has to be at the center of who we really are as a company.

Defining your sense of purpose is a liberating process. But it takes some dedication. It's an off-site exercise, requiring the full attention and best intentions of your senior staff. Get a good outside facilitator to help you plumb the depths of your organization to begin to answer questions like:

1. Besides making money, why did we get into this business in the first place?
2. What is the meaning in what we do? Can we serve a higher purpose than just providing a paycheck to our employees?
3. What kind of contribution or difference can we make in our business and in the world?

Defining your purpose is a search for the heart and soul of your business. The father of the quality movement in America, W. Edwards Deming, realized the power of a strong purpose when he listed it *number one* in his legendary "14 Points of Total Quality." He says that in order to achieve dramatic improvements in quality, you must start by creating and publishing a "statement of purpose" of the aims and purposes of the company, and that management must demonstrate their commitment to this statement.[9] That's the most important ingredient in producing a quality product.

International agency leader Jean-Marie Dru believes that a company's purpose should be both inspirational and aspirational — something that is not easily within reach. Something made not so much of goals, but of dreams. "Nothing is more powerful and motivating for companies than identifying with something they stand for and aspire to," says Dru, who has helped countless clients discover their sense of purpose.[10]

Or, as George Bernard Shaw would say, "Some men see things as they are and ask why. I dream things that never were and ask why not?"

WHAT'S THE PURPOSE OF AN ADVERTISING AGENCY?

Successful agencies have a purpose that transcends making a profit. They realize that the best people in our business don't work for money. Calvin Coolege said, "Advertising is the spiritual side of business." Former U.S. Secretary of Labor Robert Reich espouses "spiritual goals that energize an organization by resonating with the personal values of the people who work there."[11]

The people in this business who are devoted to their craft are extremely passionate about it. If they just wanted to make a lot of money, they'd take up a career in commercial real estate. As one agency concluded, "Our purpose is to make even a matchbook cover great." The purpose of GSD&M is to become what they call the MVP – Most Valuable Partner – for every one of their clients. They want to be the most important relationship a client has – more valuable than banks, accounting firms, law firms, or even materials suppliers.

Having a meaningful purpose puts you and your entire organization on a track that's difficult to derail. On the other hand, observe Hendricks and Ludeman, authors of the engaging *The Corporate Mystic,* "Without a clear sense of your purpose there are a thousand and one sidetracks to seduce you."[12]

> # Create not just a company of workers, but a company of believers.

How do you know you've reached deep enough to find your purpose?

1. It comes from inside, not outside – what you really believe, not what others think you should believe.
2. At least in some small way, it makes a contribution to something greater than just earning a living.
3. It's inspiring and motivating.

SETTING AMBITIOUS GOALS

While a goal isn't the same as a central purpose, setting ambitious goals can produce the same kind of motivation for your staff. The agencies that make their mark in this business are the ones that, as Leo Burnett used to say, "reach for the stars." Challenging goals and challenging assignments are the fuel that burns in the engines of agency superstars.

While it's important to be realistic about the strengths and weaknesses of your organization and your staff, the bigger danger lies in aiming too low. Management educators James Collins and Jerry Porras have preach the gospel of "big, hairy, audacious goals." They talk about setting personal and organizational goals that are so ambitious that they will only have a 50/50 chance of success, will require extraordinary effort, and may take a decade to fulfill. Truly motivating goals should have a "gulp factor," such as NASA's goal in the 1960s: put a man on the moon before the end of the decade.[13]

Extremely ambitious goals can a driving force that helps give your agency a sense of purpose. A modest, commonplace goal like "Achieve 20 percent profitability this year" is fine, but this is a perennial goal for every agency on the planet. To say "Move from $20 million to $200 million in billings in the next five years" paints a completely different picture. Any employee that's exposed to a goal like this clearly gets the message that this agency intends to accomplish big things.

What are some other motivating goals for agencies?

- Get a story in *Advertising Age* with the headline, "Who Are These Guys?"
- Have the agency featured in *Communications Arts*.
- Get a spot on the Super Bowl.
- Bring home three Gold Pencils in The One Show.
- Be named *Adweek's* "Agency of the Year" for your region.
- Get a cover story in *Fast Company*.
- Be ranked in the 100 best companies to work for.
- Make an unknown brand into a household name.
- Do something so outrageous that Letterman makes fun of you.

People work best and hardest when they are challenged. The risk lies not in making their jobs too big, but too small. The people who are most enthusiastic and contribute the most to the agency are the ones who are given big goals and big jobs. Give your team something to reach for, something to aspire to, and you'll light a fire that will burn in everybody.

Remember, the truly outstanding agencies are not just trying to create advertising, but in some small way change the world.

What are your agency's rules of engagement?

3 PRINCIPLES: The Lines You Draw In The Sand

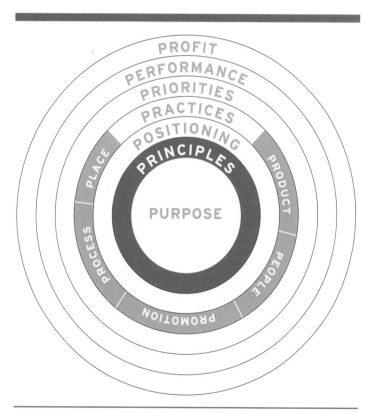

EMANATING FROM your purpose are your *principles* – a set of strongly held values that give you a framework for making business decisions. Principles are an articulation of what you will *always* do and what you will *never* do.

The most admired agencies are those that have a set of principles they follow no matter what the circumstance. They walk their talk. As advertising great Bill Bernbach said, "A principle isn't a principle until it costs you money."

Agencies with strong principles aren't afraid to say no to clients, because clients aren't the highest value. Principles are. Agencies that have principles about the quality of their work say no to unreasonable budgets and deadlines. They say no to uninformed changes to creative work and media plans.

The self-promotion literature of one prominent West Coast agency plants this flag in the ground:

> "We will *not* do everything we're told. We will make it our responsibility to bring you ideas you didn't ask for, and to keep solving problems in new and different ways. We will argue for what we believe in, but we won't be jerks about it. There are enough jerks in the world already."[1]

In times of difficult decision making, when the work of the agency might be compromised, young agency account executives are often told by agency management, "Remember, it's the client's money." This is code for "Stop fighting for what's right and just do what the client tells you or we might lose the account." In times like these, consider which is more precious: the client's money, or the agency's reputation?

Money, once lost, is fairly easy to get back. Reputation, once lost, is nearly impossible to get back. In the agency business, managers have to make little compromises virtually every day of their lives. But principle-centered managers fight like crazy to avoid making *big* compromises that can destroy what has taken years to build: their own brand image.

Perhaps the question agency managers should ask themselves is not only "How much money will this client *make* us," but "How much money will this client *cost* us – by destroying our reputation, our morale, and ultimately our ability to be successful in the future?" We all know this, but we need to be reminded: reputation is infinitely more valuable than money. And living by your principles is how you protect your reputation.

Consider which is more precious; the client's money or the agency's reputation?

Consider principles as your agency's "rules of engagement." The more your business world revolves around principles, the less likely you are to overreact to changes in the marketplace. In fact, a company shouldn't change its core values in response to market changes at all. Instead, it should consider changing markets to remain true to its core values.[2]

Otherwise, how "core" are the values?

UNCOVERING YOUR AGENCY DNA

Companies are organic entities. Embedded in every organization is a naturally-occurring strand of values and beliefs. To stay healthy, companies have to be nourished by living and staying true to these principles.

Principles are guideposts for your staff that provide the direction they need to make the hundreds of day-to-day decisions that determine the success and direction of the agency. Those that feel passionately about it, like VitroRobertson, use language like this:

> "We believe that when a group of people get together and decide to open an ad agency, that decision carries with it a group of responsibilities. The agencies that, over the long term, neglect those responsibilities and let them fall by the wayside are the agencies that will struggle and make foolish compromises and allow their creative product to erode until those agencies themselves fall by the wayside. The agencies that never lose sight of those responsibilities and that try to live up to them every day are the agencies that will be respected and do outstanding work and will prosper in even the most competitive of agency environments."[3]

To discover your principles, look deep inside your company's genetic make up and ask:

1. When it comes to business, what are the lines we draw in the sand?
2. What are the things we will always do, and the things we will never do?
3. Are we prepared to make our business decisions based on these principles?
4. Would we hold to these principles even when a significant amount of money is on the line?

THE VALUE OF VALUES

Like a good purpose, a good principle is specific and pregnant with meaning. Platitudes like "We believe in being honest" are not only not memorable, they are not defining. If you feel strongly about the subject of honesty, you might have a principle that says "We believe in telling the truth no matter what the cost." That draws a deeper line in the sand.

One of the leading principals of a well-respected New York agency believed that growth should come from a small list of strong clients. The agency – Amarati & Puris – was an example of an agency that stuck to their knitting by doing high-quality work for a select group of blue chip clients.

A smaller New York shop follows a completely different set of principles to set itself apart from the crowd. "Whenever we're uncertain which way to go," they say, "we ask ourselves what a traditional agency would do. Then we do the opposite."[4] For starters, they will work *only* on a project basis.

Principles often provoke debate and discussion. For an agency to have a section in its promotional brochure titled "What We Believe" is not very unusual. What *is* unusual is to have something concrete and provocative to say about what you believe. Most of the time, an agency's values are described with shopworn terms like "We believe in results" and "We believe in being partners with our clients." The question is, what kind of agency *doesn't* claim to believe in things like results and partnership? Deeply-rooted, well-defined principles are thought-provoking and sometimes even controversial. They give your organization character.

One agency states prominently in the first few sentences of their brochure, "We actually hate advertising. In fact, hating advertising is a prerequisite to work here." They go on to describe their belief in "advertising that doesn't look, sound, and smell like advertising." As a result, a lot of their print work looks more like magazine articles than ads, and their commercials play more like mini-movies than TV spots.[5]

Agencies must dig deep into their corporate culture to find what they *really* believe (not just what they say they believe). The agency I co-founded, Williams & Rockwood, articulated the following set of principles:

1. We believe in the value of a creative approach not only to advertising, but to every element of a client's marketing program – from strategy development to media planning.
2. We believe that it is always in our client's best interest to produce work that is truly original. Just the same, we believe that a good agency must know the rules before it can break the rules, so we devote ourselves to continually studying our craft.

3. We value honesty and candor in our advice to clients. This means presenting our recommendations with conviction based on what we believe is right for the client. At the same time, we are reasonable people who have a healthy respect for the client's knowledge and opinions.

4. We believe that by allowing people a high degree of freedom, a superior working environment is possible despite the hectic nature of our business. At Williams & Rockwood, one's time and efforts should be self-regulated to the greatest degree possible. The satisfaction that comes from a job well done is far more important than external rules and guidelines.

5. We want all of our relationships to be characterized by genuine friendliness, cooperation, and teamwork; where clients, prospective clients, suppliers, associates and even competitors are given royal treatment in every sense of the word.

6. We realize the importance of balancing work with family, health and outside interests, believing that people who lead balanced lives are happier and produce better work.

7. Above all, we want working at Williams & Rockwood to be fun, because we believe this is the environment in which creative ideas thrive.

It's important to distinguish between principles and practices. Principles are the "what," and practices are the "how." No one knows his way around the subject of principles better than best-selling author Stephen R. Covey, who offers this insight:

Clients are not the highest value. Principles are.

"If you focus on principles, you empower everyone who understands those principles to act without constant monitoring, evaluation, correcting, or controlling. Principles have universal application. And when these are internalized into habits, they empower people to create a wide variety of practices to deal with different situations."[6]

The man who built one of the most successful business enterprises in history, Dee Hock, founder of VISA International, knows firsthand the value of a common set of principles. Says Hock:

"Your organization needs to be absolutely clear about purpose and principles. If the purpose and principles are constructive and healthy, then your organization will take a very different form than anything that you ever imagined. To the degree that you hold purpose and principles in common among you, you can dispense with command and control. People will know how to behave in accordance with them, and they'll do it in thousands of unimaginable, creative ways. The organization will become a vital, living set of beliefs."[7]

Imagine that kind of alignment taking place in your agency.

THE POWER OF A POINT OF VIEW

The best agencies have a strong, well-articulated philosophy. They put it in writing, and they go to great lengths to make sure everyone on their staff understands and embraces it. One of the best-known examples of this stems from the early years of Ogilvy & Mather. A series of O&M philosophy pieces were used religiously in agency training, new business, and self promotion. Titles like these clearly paint a picture of an agency with an opinion:

How to Create Advertising That Sells
How to Launch New Products
How to Advertise Travel
How to Make Successful Television Commercials
How to Make Your Sales Promotions More Profitable
How to Create Corporate Advertising That Gets Results
How to Run an Advertising Agency
How to Make Agency Presentations
How to Write Better

You may agree or disagree with what David Ogilvy had to say about the advertising business, but you've got to give him credit for having a point of view. During its first 25 years, O&M was propelled from a start-up agency to one of the largest in the world, fueled by a strong philosophy that made the agency famous. In writing his "Principles of Management," David Ogilvy said, "If you endorse these principles, promulgate them, apply them, add to them and revise them during the years to come, our offices will be inspired by unanimity of purpose. This will give Ogilvy &

Mather a competitive edge over international agencies which lack such unanimity."[8] He was right.

O&M is perhaps the best-known example of an agency with strong principles. They run deep in the collective soul of the organization. David Ogilvy, in his trademark colorful style, put most of the agency's principles in writing, including these:[9]

1. We admire people who hire subordinates who are good enough to succeed them. We pity people who are so insecure that they feel compelled to hire inferior specimens as their subordinates.
2. We admire kindly people with gentle manners who treat other people as human beings – particularly the people who sell things to us. We abhor quarrelsome people. We abhor people who wage paper warfare. We abhor buck passers, and people who don't tell the truth.
3. Our system of management is singularly democratic. We don't like hierarchical bureaucracy or rigid pecking orders.
4. We despise office politicians, toadies, bullies and pompous asses. We detest nepotism and every other form of favoritism.
5. We attach importance to discretion. Clients don't appreciate agencies which leak their secrets. Nor do they like it when an agency takes credit for their successes. To get between a client and the footlights is bad manners.
6. We are revolted by pseudo-academic jargon, like attitudinal, paradigms, demassification, reconceptualize, suboptimal, symbiotic linkage, splinterisation, and dimensionalisation.
7. We use the word partner in referring to each other. This says a mouthful.
8. We admire well-organized people who keep their offices shipshape, and deliver their work on time.

When strong principles seep through the collective consciousness of an agency, they serve as a set of boundaries that guide daily decisions. One of the true professionals I have known in this business, creative director Dave Newbold, once committed some of his agency's principles on paper as follows:[10]

1. We are dedicated to making creativity the horse and billings the cart. Not vice versa.
2. We only work for clients who seek honest, objective input, who decry "yes" folks, and who value partners with spines.

3. We cannot work for everyone. We will resist the temptation. Our agency must and will position itself based on our strengths and experience, then pursue only clients whose needs match those attributes.
4. We will not accept a client that has a system which deters creativity and risk-taking, or which has multiple levels of approval.
5. We must care. A lot. Advertising *is* brain surgery. The work matters. The ideas matter. The execution matters. It makes a difference how the headline is worded, how big the type and how small the logo is.
6. All members of the agency are, first and foremost, accountable for the creative excellence and reputation of the agency.
7. We will not permit "closet" accounts. If the work is not good enough to show new business prospects, the account is not good enough to keep.

Clients respect a strong, even controversial point of view. Bartle Bogle Hegarty is famous for a set of principles that have contributed not only to their stellar reputation, but ultimately to their bottom line. When BBH first opened for business, they announced their policy of refusing to prepare speculative creative work in new business pitches. London papers like the *Financial Times* and *The Observer* called it "A potentially suicidal policy," and "A recipe for disaster." Much to the contrary, BBH has one of the best new business conversion rates of any agency anywhere. Other BBH principles astound and confound, such as the agency's policy of presenting only one creative option to the client at a time. And when it comes to client compensation, they have only one approach: theirs. You can argue with these policies, but you can't argue with their success; BBH is an agency brand in demand. And their principles are a big part of it. As New York office chairman Cindy Gallop says, "There's real strength in saying 'We're not for everybody.'"

It's an observable fact that principle-centered agencies seem to have certain things (principles, actually) in common. Of course, agencies have their own personalities and cultures, but the best of them tend to share a set of recurring values. Here are a few of the most important ones.

VALUING GREATNESS OVER BIGNESS

"Grow or die." This is a classic principle, deeply embedded in the American business psyche. Agencies, like other businesses, are obsessed with size. Eavesdrop on any elevator conversation between executives of different agencies and the first question will be, "So, how big are you guys now?" The question should be, "So how *good* are you guys now?"

What exactly is the benefit of growth for the sake of growth? In a creative enterprise like an agency, you can either care about great work, great people, and great clients, which usually results in growth. Or you can care about growth, which only *sometimes* results in great work, great people, and great clients.

Bigness does not lead to greatness.

As Wieden + Kenney co-founder Dan Wieden observed, "At the end of the day, size and scale isn't king, relationship is king. And getting bigger doesn't make relationships easier, it makes them much more difficult."[11]

Minneapolis-based Carmichael Lynch has grown with the same philosophy. The agency's Jack Supple once said, "We're probably the only agency in America not looking for a big client."[12] He wants the agency to grow carefully – not quickly – in a way that's aligned with the agency's principles.

"We've been accused of screening our clients, and I think that's true," says Martin Puris, co-founder of the now-legendary Amarati Puris. "I don't think that every client is for us or we're the agency for every client. Maybe the difference between us and everybody else is that we're not afraid to say so."[13]

New York agency Kirshenbaum & Bond has a similar view. Says partner Richard Kirshenbaum, "My personal philosophy has never been about getting bigger. It's always been about getting better. And every time we've ever tried to get better, we've got bigger."[14]

Are these aggressive growth philosophies? Not on the surface. But have these agencies grown anyway? Quite impressively.

WHEN LESS IS MORE

I know of one small agency that felt they were constantly running to keep up the demands of 24 clients. Then one day the partners made the decision that they would muster the courage to say goodbye to the accounts that weren't adding much to the agency's income or reputation and cut their client list in half – down to 12. They immediately lost hundreds of thousands of dollars in income. But in less than a year the agency literally doubled in size.

A well-known and much larger agency in the Southwestern U.S. had a similar experience. In the 1980s, the agency had grown to four offices, spreading the time and attention of the founders among too many locations and too many clients. The agency made the brave decision to close all but the headquarters office, which required them to resign two-thirds of their clients. The agency billed about $60 million at the time. Today (with just one office), they bill well over $1 billion.

Why? Because by focusing on what they did best, they were more efficient, more effective, and more profitable than trying to be everything to everyone. Being focused proves the old adage, "Sometimes less is more."

TAMING THE CORPORATE EGO

After many years of observing successful companies, *Good to Great* author Jim Collins issues this warning: "Never think of your company as great, no matter how successful it becomes."[15] After winning a few big accounts or a few big awards, the biggest threat to an agency living its principles is getting caught up in its own "greatness." Advertising people have such healthy egos that it happens all the time.

Some observers call this "CEO disease," and it's particularly bad among ad agencies. The cause of this malady is lack of self-awareness. The higher up you go in an organization, the less the self-awareness. Many leaders and managers have a highly inaccurate understanding of how others view their actions and behavior. In fact, the poorer the manager, the greater the chance that manager believes he or she is doing a good job. It's an interesting phenomenon that the best managers tend to rate their performance lower than the worst managers. That's because better managers have better self-awareness.[16]

Great agencies don't believe their own press. David Ogilvy used to say, "We have a habit of divine discontent with our performance. It is an antidote to smugness." Tom McElligott of the once-named Fallon McElligott believed that "When egos start getting fat and happy, creativity starts to get thin and pale." When you walk into the offices of today's Fallon, there are no conspicuous trophy cases displaying the agency's many awards.

In a piece about Mike Hughes's brilliant leadership of The Martin Agency, *Adweek* calls Hughes' style the kind of leadership that can never be satisfied. "Praise his ads," they say, "and he'll tell you they should have been better. Hand him a gold One Show Pencil, and he'll fret over the work that isn't as good. Point out how much the agency has grown, and he can only talk about what hasn't been done."[17] A healthy dose of humility can go a long way.

GOOD ENOUGH IS NOT GOOD ENOUGH

When I worked on the Mrs. Fields Cookies account, I was impressed by the corporate mantra, which was prominently displayed on plaques throughout the company's offices. It reads, "Good enough is not good enough."

MORE PRINCIPLES WITH PRINCIPLE

For further inspiration on the subject of principles, consider a few more real-life examples from agencies that value their values.

- We will only seek relationships with clients who want what we can deliver. We will never try and fake our way through weaknesses.
- We hate hierarchy. We believe in a flat organizational structure that puts the work first.
- We believe in hard work, but we will always defend our right to lead a balanced life.
- We reject the notion that bigger is better. Better is better
- We prize having a higher degree of civility in our client and peer-to-peer relationships than other agencies.
- We will always be on the leading edge (but not bleeding edge) of technology. We believe the purpose of technology is to free us up to do what humans do best – think.
- We believe nothing is more important than trust. We will avoid speaking negatively about each other, our clients, or our competition – especially behind their backs.
- We will always value effectiveness over efficiency. Efficiency by itself, unless it contributes a meaningful outcome, is worthless.
- We will maintain an organization where the principals of the company are personally involved in the business of every client, even if this means limiting the number of clients the agency will accept.
- We are trusted stewards of our client's money. We feel so strongly about this that we have systems that actively reward people who save money for our clients. Our books are open to our clients at all times and without advance notice.

Even more thought provoking is the plaque I saw one morning in an agency principal's office, which said, "Good is the enemy of great." His philosophy is that he shouldn't support good work. He should support *great* work. To him, the psychological difference is significant. When I have conducted interviews with employees at agencies with stellar creative reputations, I have usually heard them say something like, "The partners here are perfectionists." I ask, "Does that drive you crazy?" "No," they say, "it just makes us work harder to try and hit a home run. Otherwise, the partners will just send us back to bat again." It's no coincidence that these are the kinds of agencies where the work is not just good, but great.

When it comes to quality of work, good is the enemy of great.

Agencies that have *great* (instead of good) as one of their principles don't tolerate sloppy work, sloppy service, or sloppy thinking. They don't do one round of color, they do five. They're rarely satisfied with the first edit. They rewrite their marketing plans. And they keep trying to make everything better right up until the moment the work goes out the door.

Bill Marsteller, founder of the respected Marsteller agency was adamant about refusing to live with bad or ordinary work:

> "Even if work that doesn't meet our standards somehow gets through, until an ad is actually bound into a publication or a commercial is on the air, it may not be too late to change it. Try. A client will respect you for attempting to improve an ad, even if he already approved it. Admittedly, redoing, reshooting, reselling all take time. Often overtime. They take effort. They take persuasion, friendly and otherwise. They take guts. But they're almost always worth it. Who's responsible for making sure only our best work is produced? Anyone. Everyone. You. And how do you know when it's our best work? You know. There's a little voice inside that tells you. Listen to it."[18]

Stanley Pollitt, founder of a London agency and widely considered to be the father of the discipline of account planning, said that "Success means a total agency management commitment to getting the advertising right at all costs. It's more important than maximizing agency profits or keeping clients happy."[19] What a standard for an agency to live up to. These words would no doubt send cold chills down the spines of many agency presidents, client service directors, and new business directors, but what Pollitt was advocating was that if you get the advertising right, the rest will follow naturally.

Devotion to the work starts at the top. When you personally commit to getting it right and making it great, your staff will follow willingly in your footsteps.

NOTHING TO HIDE

How many agencies do you know who reward their people by letting them work on the "showcase" accounts? The first question to ask is "Should agencies even *have* showcase accounts?" What kind of message does it send when you have "bread-and-butter" accounts (the kind that "pay the bills around here"), and another class of "showcase" accounts?

I recall a sunny California morning when I was meeting with a small but principle-centered agency with a national reputation for stellar creative work. To give me an overview of their agency, the partners ran though a presentation showing the strategy, the creative work, and the results for about five clients. At the end of their presentation I said, "That's fabulous work. Now tell me about the rest of your clients." They said, "That's it. That's all of our clients. In fact, we've shown you every single piece of work we did this year for every single one of our clients." The work they had shown me ranged from television spots to tray liners, and it was *all* great.

Now there are two things that are unusual about this. First, any other agency this size (they had about 20 people) would have at least 20 clients. They had five. Second, most agencies have a combination of "showcase" accounts and "bread and butter" accounts. Not this one.

As one well-respected agency principal once said, "You can measure our agency by the clients we *don't* have."

WALKING THE TALK

Socrates said, "The way to gain a good reputation is to endeavor to be what you desire to appear." Said another way, to be successful, we must align our practices with our principles.

When it comes down to it, the real difference between truly outstanding agencies and everybody else is that they not only talk the talk, they actually *walk the walk*. They have a strong alignment between what they say and what they do, between principles and practices. My friend and long-time agency executive Charlie Decker wrote a book titled *99 Principles and Practices of Procter & Gamble's Success*. His conclusion? "Many business decisions have effects that go beyond beating the competition or making a profit. It often comes down to the hard choice between what's right for the long term versus the short term. If decisions are inconsistent with principles, the principles will ultimately be undermined."[20]

It all boils down to two important questions:

1. Does our agency have a set of principles which guide every business decision?
2. Are our policies, procedures, and daily practices aligned with our principles?

If you answer no to either of these questions, involve your agency in some serious self-reflection. And remember that you don't invent your guiding principles, you *discover* them. They're in there, just waiting to come out. Find them, put them in writing, and emblazon them on the agency consciousness. When you walk into the entrance of GSD&M in Austin, you find their principles literally carved in stone – in the granite floor of the lobby.

It's time to recreate our "all things to all people" mission statements and decide what it is we really stand for – the things we will always do and the things we will never do. Most importantly, we must remember that the most dangerous course of action is inaction. Remember the advice of the German philosopher Goethe: "Things which matter most must never be at the mercy of things which matter least."

How can you focus your agency to attract more of the people and clients you really want?

4 POSITIONING:
Making The Most Of Your Point Of Difference

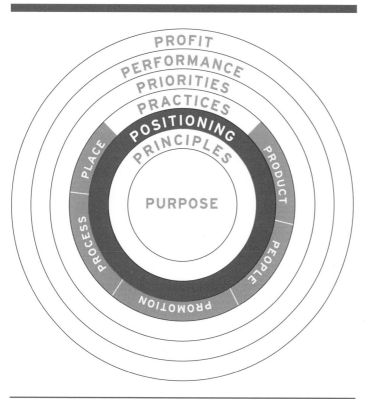

"IF WE DON'T DO IT, someone else will." How many times have you heard this phrase uttered in the hallways of the agency? This kind of thinking can otherwise be interpreted as, "We'd better provide every possible service our client will ever need, or they'll fire us and hire another agency that can."

This form of paranoia cannot only hurt the agency; it can hurt the client as well. It hurts the client because the agency pretends to be able to do everything from sports marketing to Web sites, but does actually very little of it very well. It hurts the agency because instead of being known for doing *something* well, the agency becomes just another of the thousands of "full-service integrated marketing communications firms."

Take a look at your competitors' self-promotion literature and you'll soon come to the conclusion that most of it looks and sounds remarkably alike. When it comes to inside-out thinking, advertising agencies are as guilty as their clients. Agencies constantly scold their clients for being too "product-centric" and tell them that they should motivate their customers by promising one single benefit rather than rattling off a list of product features; yet *agency* literature is typically packed with lists of product features – agency services, agency size, agency structure, agency history, agency functions, agency departments. Not a very compelling approach for experts in marketing.

Most agencies promise to do everything, the list of bullet points virtually never-ending. They are so anxious to try to meet every client need that they don't realize that it actually *decreases* trust when you try to tap dance, and *increases* client trust when you tell them you can't do something. Seems like it should be the other way around, doesn't it?

An excellent example of doing what you do best is found in the history of a small but very talented agency in Jackson Hole, Wyoming that started as Riddell Advertising & Design. Years ago, founder Ed Riddell was smart enough to know that Jackson Hole isn't exactly the center of the advertising universe, and that Wyoming clients are few and far between. Riddell needed to be able to give prospective clients a reason why they should get on a plane from another state and work with an agency in – of all places – Jackson Hole.

Based on work they had done over the years in categories like mountain bikes, goggles, and fishing and climbing equipment, Ed Riddell thought to himself, "We've created a marketing position for many of our clients; why not create one for ourselves?" So the agency carved out a niche as an outdoor sports specialist. Ed Riddell realized that a lot of his staff moved to Wyoming so they could ski, hike, and bike. That kind of interest and experience gave the agency a natural edge that helped them attract clients from far beyond the borders of Wyoming.[1] Considering the growth in popularity of outdoor activities that is sweeping the U.S., it was a pretty smart decision.

STANDING FOR SOMETHING

I once heard a story about a stretch of highway in North Dakota that goes in a straight line for 40 miles. If you drive this long, lonely road at night, you experience what the locals call "white line fever." After 10 miles or so, the white dividing lines take on a mesmerizing quality, and you begin to drift to the middle of the road just to stay awake. Most agency brands have this tendency – to move to the middle. To be in the middle is to have no position at all. As positioning authority Al Ries preaches, "Narrowing your focus and being strong somewhere is a better approach than expanding your focus and winding up weak everywhere."[2]

Not too long ago, National Public Radio reported on a study done by the U.S. television industry to find out what really determines success in local TV news ratings. Using a set of common criteria, stations in several cities around the country were assigned grades from A to F. Curiously, the stations that got the highest viewership were those who received A and F grades. The ones in the middle – the stations that received B, C and D grades – all lagged behind in viewership. Why? Because the A and F stations clearly stood for something. The stations that received A grades stood for a serious, information-based approach to news. The stations graded F represented a more celebrity-driven "infotainment" tabloid approach to news. The stations graded B, C and D stood for nothing unusual – like a lot of traditional full service agencies – and barely showed up on the viewership ratings.[3]

This same phenomenon can be applied to the agency world. The agencies that are known for something draw the attention, while everybody else is very unmemorably in the middle.

A recent study by MIT's Ezra Zuckerman turned up a similar pattern in the world of movies. For most actors who get a film credit, it takes an average of three years to land their next contract. But for actors who are willing to be identified with a particular genre, assignments come much faster and more consistently. The moral? "If you start off as a generalist and try to avoid typecasting," observes Zuckerman, "you may not get to play in the first place."[4]

Branding your agency means moving from the middle and taking a side. It means realizing that you can't "boil the ocean." If you don't claim a position, you will be positioned simply by your location. Which is really no position at all.

DISTINCT VS. EXTINCT

While agencies preach differentiation, most behave like commodities. The oft-quoted Harvard professor Theodore Leavitt believes no company should be or behave like a commodity. "Differentiation," he says, "is one of the most important strategic and tactical activities in which companies must constantly engage. There is no such thing as a commodity, only people who act and think like commodities. Everything can be differentiated." [5]

While agencies preach differentiation, most behave like commodities.

As a starting point, consider what has made your agency successful up to this point. Is it a reputation for brilliant print advertising? Exceptional strategic planning and research? Great interactive work? Strong media clout? Unusual experience in retail advertising?

Now ponder a few more questions:

1. What kind of clients have you been most successful in attracting in the past?
2. In what areas do you have superior knowledge or expertise?
3. What do you do particularly well, perhaps better than most other agencies?
4. What do you most enjoy doing? What do you hate doing?
5. What business are you really in?
6. What's the one thing your agency is most known for?
7. What kind of focus would you choose if you were starting this agency for the first time?

To save some time, let's define up front what *doesn't* qualify as a strong agency positioning.

> Full service
> Integrated
> Quality creative work
> Excellent client service
> Results oriented

Believe it or not, these are the most popular agency "positionings" in the world today. Problem is, they really aren't positionings.

Positioning expert Jack Trout makes the same observation. He says:[6]

> Quality and customer orientation are rarely differentiating ideas.
> Creativity is not a differentiating idea.
> Price is rarely a differentiating idea.
> Breadth of line is a difficult way to differentiate.

Let's look at a few *actual* agency positionings to see if they qualify as differentiating:

> "To create powerful ideas that build business for clients that are driven to win." (This might be motivating, but it is hardly differentiating. Pretty much any agency could say it – and most do.)

> "To produce brilliant work that generates success for aggressive intelligent clients using the power of creativity."(Same problem.)

> "To provide top-notch work to top-notch companies." (Hmmm, this is starting to sound familiar.)

It's no wonder clients have a difficult time distinguishing one agency from another when the stacks of agency literature pile up in their offices during an agency review. Agency search consultant Michael Marsak calls this "the sea of sameness" among advertising agencies.[7] Some clients believe that if you've read one agency brochure, you've read them all. And with agency descriptions like this (quoted from an actual agency brochure), they may be right:

> "(Your name goes here) is a marketing communications company that provides its clients with a broad range of integrated marketing disciplines. The highest priority is placed on developing and sustaining relationships with clients, understanding their objectives, and partnering with them to achieve their goals."

Once again, with feeling: this is *not* a positioning. It's merely a description of an agency that's a mile wide and only a few inches deep.

BASIC POSITIONING OPTIONS FOR AGENCIES

To move from platitudes to positioning, consider that at a very basic level, agencies can define a position for themselves in at least one of three basic ways:

1. Focusing on a discipline.
2. Focusing on a category.
3. Focusing on an audience.

Focusing on a Discipline

One of the most obvious (but also most effective) ways to focus a marketing communications organization is on a *discipline*. Direct marketing has long been a specialty, as has sales promotion, recruitment advertising, public relations and design. Since 1990, interactive agencies have appeared on the scene. And most recently, the phenomenon of "brand consultancies."

Some more unusual variations of focusing on a discipline are the agencies that do "creative only" (no media departments), "ideas only" (like Brighthouse in Atlanta), "relationship marketing" (a more comprehensive approach to traditional direct marketing), and "digital marketing" (a new way to title interactive specialists), and "rapid response" (quick turnaround project specialists)

For the agencies that have chosen the path of specialization, the success stories are huge.

Focusing on a Category

The agencies that have built a skill set around a particular *category* of business have also found it easier to compete nationally than the typical agency that tries to be all things to all people. Agency experts can be found in business-to-business, health care, pharmaceuticals, retail, entertainment, fashion, travel, real estate, financial services, retail advertising, high technology, and even "urban marketing." Some agencies (especially in Washington D.C.) concentrate on issues advertising.

After spending his career with large New York agencies, my former boss and mentor, Ted French, became a partner in a firm with a category focus. "We are a full service agency that specializes in business-to-business accounts," said Ted in describing his agency. "We specialize because business-to-business is where we have something exceptional to offer. We avoid areas where we do not have special expertise."[8] It's pretty hard to argue with that kind of logic.

If you're located in a smaller market, think of the appeal you would have to some clients outside your geographical area if you built a specialization in "natural products," as an agency in Salt Lake City does. Makers of herbal supplements, homeopathic remedies, organic foods, and other natural products from all over the world seek out this small but focused agency.

An acquaintance of mine in Philadelphia, Ed Tettemer, runs a remarkably successful agency that focuses exclusively on cable TV brands. You may argue that's a very narrow niche, but that's exactly what makes them a thriving enterprise. The agency, Red Tettemer, calls itself "The communications company for communications and entertainment companies." A recent headline in the Philadelphia

IS "CREATIVITY" A POSITIONING?

It seems that since agencies are in the business of creativity that a reputation for creative work should be something most agencies have in common. But they don't. Just as some architectural firms are excellent in engineering but only average in design, a lot of agencies are terrific at client service but mediocre in creative execution. Which means the agencies that are fully devoted to outstanding creative work really do stand out. In fact, they are most often the agency names that come to mind when you think of "agency brands."

Despite the fact that only a handful of agencies have earned recognition as creative leaders, virtually every agency claims creative leadership. This is one of the main reasons agencies tend to look and sound alike to prospective clients, and why the promise of "killer creative" has lost its meaning. (To add to the irony, the agencies that really are creative leaders rarely claim to be.) Nordstrom, the department store with far and away the best service, never brags about service.

So is creativity a point of difference? Yes, but a dangerous one. Only a few agencies can rightfully claim it, and most of those who can, don't.

Business Journal tells it all: "One for the contrarians: Ad agency is expanding." The story explains that while other Philadelphia firms are laying off staff and closing offices, Red Tettemer is hiring people in all disciplines. Even during the worst advertising industry recession since the Great Depression, the agency doubled its staff and has had revenue increases of 30 percent annually since it was founded in 1996. "We made a deliberate decision to focus," says Ed Tettemer. Their decision has made them the country's leading agency for entertainment and communications brands.

You may argue that these kinds of specialists are not the largest agencies. Maybe not. They are, however, some of the most profitable.

Focusing on an Audience

Yet another twist on the ways agencies can focus is to develop core competencies around a particular *audience*. There are agencies that specialize in marketing to women, seniors, youth, Latinos, African-Americans, Asians, and outdoor enthusiasts. Some agencies have built a reputation by mostly representing brands that appeal to "the affluent." A successful agency in Portland, Oregon, built its business based on an expertise in a very specialized but influential audience: engineers. Even large agencies are following suit; McCann-Erickson has a unit that specializes in marketing to 18-24 year-olds.

Focusing on an audience is a particularly powerful form of positioning, because it allows you to become expert in understanding the attitudes, values, habits, wants, needs, motivations, and behavior of a particular class of people. This in-depth knowledge is infinitely attractive to companies who market their products to the audience you have chosen.

Other Positionings

Sometimes the best – and most unusual – positionings come from combining some of the above elements in unconventional ways. For example, an agency in San Diego is positioned around "active lifestyles." They represent products and services that range from golf to resort hotels to sports nutrition bars. An agency in the Northeast developed a similar focus, but named their specialty "Play."

Another agency examined their core competencies and discovered that with all their retail experience, what they're really good at is "driving traffic." More specifically, "driving traffic to physical locations where consumers make a purchase." This kind of positioning doesn't restrict the agency to any given discipline, category, or audience; but it does differentiate them from the thousands of other agencies who claim to do everything.

Sometimes agency brands can be built on a strong point of view. A very talented copywriter in the Pacific Northwest decided to take the plunge into the agency business and formed a unique agency named FourStories. The vision of FourStories, according to founder Austin Howe, is about "focusing our ambition energies on four brands we love." His plan is to take on four – and only four – clients of similar size and values and then grow those companies. How's that for a brave concept?[9]

Another example of a successful positioning built on a strong philosophy is the natural products company Tom's of Maine. Here's a company that doesn't see every adult in the world as a potential customer. Instead, they focus on those who share their respect for the environment. CEO Tom Chappell reminds his employees that they are not selling soap; they are selling *natural ingredients*. Their commitment to nature is what sets the company apart. Customers buy their products because they share the company's values and like what the company does for the environment and the community.[10]

A distinctive attitude can work in similar ways for agencies. Agency search consultant Russel Wohlwerth observed that one very notable New York agency is distinctive because "they always tell it like it is, regardless of whether the client wants to hear it or not. They're obsessed with results the same way some agencies are obsessed with awards. Some agencies disregard what the client wants or likes in order to get awards. This agency is willing to disregard what the client wants or likes in order to get *results*." Now that's attitude.

ONE AGENCY'S PROCESS OF DISCOVERY

An agency with a decade-long track record led their management team through the process of discovering their positioning. They started by developing a list of "common threads," in which they asked themselves, "How could we characterize our collective experience with clients and brands over the past 10 years."

Here's what they found:

- Primarily marketing to consumers
- Primarily retail advertising
- Primarily companies who need to drive sales and short-term results
- Primarily products that are "consumed"

From this came a key insight. The agency team realized that most of the brands they had worked on over the years are products people *crave*. This led them to a positioning that played squarely on their distinctive strengths: "We build brands that consumers 'gotta have.'" This doesn't mean all brands – it means only brands that evoke an emotional, sensory *craving*. Marketing *impulse brands* is what this agency does best, so that's where they decided to put their considerable energies.

Their new business list was revised to focus on "gotta have" categories like fashion, food, beverages, entertainment, recreation, and other impulse brands. Deciding to focus on "brands people crave" gave this agency a differentiating position in the crowded agency marketplace. It also gave them a focal point around which they aligned their practices – product, people, process, promotion, and place.

In some instances, the agency brand is a result of a strong, distinctive leader. Agency leaders like David Ogilvy, Leo Burnett, and Bill Bernbach cast long shadows that created memorable reputations for their agencies. Although this is a much rarer phenomenon today, figures like Stan Richards, Jim Mullen, and Donny Deutsch have been the defining factor for their respective agencies.

If you want to really think outside the box, consider how a Scottish agency named Faulds approached positioning. They divided their agency up into five different brands. Clients could pick any one of the following, depending on their needs:

Classic Faulds	Traditional advertising accounts
Total Faulds	Integrated marketing solutions
Fast Faulds	Retail and fast-turnaround advertising
Media Faulds	Media-only business
Future Faulds	Brand consulting

But let's get back to basics. One positioning for one agency is best. And finding and exploring that positioning is one of the most important and rewarding experiences an agency executive can have. You've spent your entire career working on other people's brands. Now here's a chance to work on your one of your very own.

DISCOVERING YOUR POSITION

To begin to explore a positioning for your agency, gather your senior staff together and make a list on the board labeled "What We Do." Name all the things the agency does. Now edit the list and leave only the things that you do *well*. Don't be tempted to list all the things that you attempt to do, but don't really have the necessary expertise or experience. You may end up with a pretty short list, but not only is that O.K. – it's good.

Next to your list of "What We Do," develop another list titled "What We Don't Do." Here's where you must be ultra candid. For example, you've attempted to develop a website a time or two, but you can't really call yourselves web developers. Put "web development" on the "don't do" list. In this process, you'll find yourself moving a lot of what you originally listed under "What We Do" to "What We Don't Do."

You must be ruthless in how you think about your agency strengths. Don't list "direct response" as a strength just because you've produced a few postcard mailings for clients. You're looking for natural strengths here — the things you do well and do consistently.

If the "What We Do" list is three times longer than the "What We Don't Do" list, start over. You're missing the point of positioning. Go back and move some of the "Do" items to "Don't Do." Here's an actual example from an agency that engaged in this process of self-discovery:

What We Do	What We Don't Do
Consumer insights using account planning	Interactive
Advertising concept development and production	Internet marketing and E-commerce
Collateral development	Design
Point-of-sale	Direct response and database marketing
Sales promotion	Investor relations
Mass media planning and placement	Trade shows and exhibits
Media relations	Events and sponsorships
Community relations	Corporate communications
Building consumer brands	Public affairs

As you sit back and look at your "What We Do" list, you'll see that it's really a list of core competencies of the agency. You shouldn't feel that just because you don't have "broadcast media planning and buying" listed as a core competency that somehow you're deficient. It's probably a result of the fact that you do a lot of business-to-business advertising, and you work mostly in print. That's just fine. You don't need to "round out" your agency by trying to do everything in the book. The point is to be clear about what you do well. And remember that growth doesn't come from doing more things, but from doing more of what you're good at already.

PUTTING IT DOWN ON PAPER

There are many different ways to frame an agency positioning; but no matter what the form, a good description of your positioning should answer four questions about your agency:

1. Who you are
2. What you are
3. What you do
4. Who you do it for

Here's an example.

Who you are	The James Gang
What you are	We are a brand communications firm.
What you do	We market travel and entertainment experiences – the experience of making a trip, going to a destination, visiting an attraction, staying in a hotel, frequenting a restaurant, etc.
Who you do it for	We work for travel and entertainment brands – destinations, hotels, resorts, airlines, rental car companies, cruise lines, restaurant chains, theme parks, etc.

You should be able to describe your positioning both within a moment's notice and within a moment. It's like the advice the respected copywriter Luke Sullivan gives to other writers who have the task of describing their client's product:

> "It's as if you're riding down an elevator with your customer. You're going down only 15 floors. So you have only a few seconds to tell him one thing about your product. One thing. And you have to tell it to him in such an interesting way that he thinks about the promise you've made as he leaves the building, waits for the light, and crosses the street."[11]

Actually, you should develop a description of your positioning in three different lengths: a sentence, a paragraph, and a page. Former President Bill Clinton used this approach when campaigning. He believed that a successful candidate should be able to describe his position on the issues in a 30-second sound bite, a five-minute stump speech, and a 30-minute dinner address. An agency needs the *sentence version* of its positioning for its website home page, the *paragraph version* for a directory listing, and the *page version* for the beginning of its agency brochure.

TAKING YOUR OWN MEDICINE

"Defining a distinctive brand is fine for other agencies," you say, "but impractical for us." Think about the advice you'd give a client who tells you they want to market their products to everybody, everywhere. You'd insist that your client be more specific, and you'd remind them that to be successful a brand has to be uniquely positioned in the mind of the consumer.

You'd insist on developing a creative brief for your client that spells out a specific objective, a specific target audience, and specific key benefits. It only stands to reason that you should apply the same standard to your agency.

If you're still not convinced that you can make your agency different, consider the fact that there are now literally hundreds of brands of the ultimate commodity: water. From Evian to Fuji, many carry a premium price, vivid brand associations, and strong brand preference. If branding works for water, it can certainly work for a professional services firm.

Think of it this way. Which would you rather count on for your success: positioning or probability? "If you don't know where you're going, you'll end up someplace else," said Yogi Berra. Said another way, if you don't have a branding strategy, you'll become part of someone else's.

> **If branding can work for water, it can work for a professional services firm.**

THE SECRET WEAPON IN NEW BUSINESS

Agencies live and die on new business. The question is, do you want to keep chasing new business or would you like to have some of it start chasing you? When clients know who you are and what you stand for, they seek *you* out. Otherwise, you're just another "full service integrated marketing communications firm." Which would you rather be?

In making branding decisions about your agency, remember that the goal is to be relentlessly focused. But being unfocused in new business is the leading sin among even experienced agency managers. When accounts are on the loose, most agencies can't resist the temptation to send their armies out to the east, the west, the north, and the south, only to find that their troops are spread too thin to win any of the battles, much less the war.

The most focused agencies are pathologically picky when it comes to new business. This allows them to be remarkably focused, and therefore remarkably successful. This goes against the conventional agency wisdom that new business is a "numbers game," that new business wins are a function of the "number of times at bat." It's a great theory. It's just that it's not completely true. The agencies that are most successful in new business are focused on clients that match their positioning.

Chinese philosopher Sun Tzu, author of the *Art of War*, teaches that if you are positioned correctly, you will actually win *before* you fight.[12] In the new business wars, clearly defined agency brands choose their battles wisely, concentrate their forces, and win.

ALIGNING THE AGENCY BRAND

PRACTICES:
Aligning The Agency Brand

YOU'VE MADE THE all-important decision about positioning. Now comes the really hard part: aligning your positioning with your practices. Through your practices, you bring your agency brand to life. Your purpose, principles, and positioning point the way to your destination. But your practices are how you get there.

When it comes to aligning your practices with your positioning, consistency is the key. "If the Richards Group produces a wonderful product but treats its employees like pond scum," says Stan Richards, "I haven't got a mere operational problem. I've got a branding problem – different promises at different points of contact with the brand."[1]

Effectively managing your agency brand means realizing that everything you do or say communicates something about your brand. Even what you don't do or say sends a message. And every brand message – intended or unintended – either strengthens or weakens your brand.

Bringing your brand to life in your daily practices can have a profound impact on your business. Researchers have actually proven a link between hard business results and the soft "feel" of a company. Getting people to rally around a common cause can improve business performance by 20 to 30 percent.[2] The investment you make in developing your agency brand can literally pay off.

So here's a more detailed look at what's needed to effectively align your practices with your positioning in five key areas:

- Product
- People
- Promotion
- Process
- Place

What changes should you make to your products, services, and capabilities to help bring your positioning to life?

5 PRODUCT: Doing What You Do Best

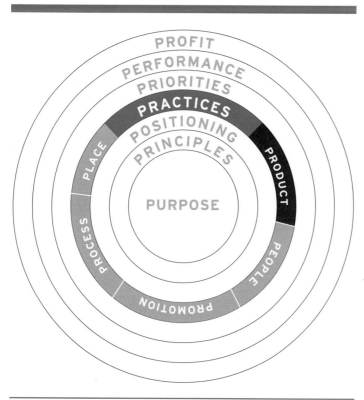

PROFIT
PERFORMANCE
PRIORITIES
PRACTICES
POSITIONING
PRINCIPLES
PLACE
PROCESS
PURPOSE
PRODUCT
PEOPLE
PROMOTION

WHAT EXACTLY DO advertising agencies have to sell? The answer to this question isn't as obvious as it seems. In the end, agencies don't sell advertising or campaigns – they sell the promise of results. But beyond delivering results for your clients, your product line-up should also be a reflection of your agency brand.

Do your products and services support your positioning and where you're trying to take your agency? Let's look at some of the critical questions.

1 **New or special capabilities.** *To fully deliver on our agency brand, what is lacking from our mix of products and services? What special or unique capabilities do we need to serve the clients in our area of focus?*

Let's say you have committed to be a business-to-business agency. That's what you know best, what you do best, and what you like best. You're now going to commit the physical and emotional resources to bring your agency brand to life. You gather your senior team for a retreat at a mountain resort for a soul-searching discussion about aligning the agency's "product" with its positioning, and discover that if you're going to be a leading B-to-B agency, you're actually missing a few capabilities that would be important to B-to-B clients. For example, you have virtually no ability to help your clients in the area of trade shows, which for many of your clients is a critically important source of leads and business. You do great business-to-business advertising, but when it comes to designing and producing trade show exhibits, you always have to outsource. Is this something you should consider doing in-house? Should this be a core competency of a serious B-to-B agency?

One of the large independent agencies in the western U.S. discovered that they could be most successful by focusing in the area where they have the most experience: travel and tourism. They decided to analyze their "product" to determine where they might need to add services that would be particularly important to tourism clients. What they found was that while they were strong in the traditional advertising disciplines, they were lacking in one area that is of prime importance to clients like hotels, airlines, and destinations: database marketing. Travel and tourism clients need to identify and market to their best customers. Developing a serious database marketing capability became one of the key initiatives for this agency.

Another agency with a focus on the technology category has yet a different product mix. For starters, they have an account management structure that complements the "marcom" structure of technology company marketing departments. They have a streamlined creative and production process that turns work around on high tech timeframes. They have a strong Internet marketing capability, a stellar IT department, and strategic alliances with "back-end" technology partners. As you might expect, this agency has memberships in technology-oriented organizations and associations. They subscribe to all the major technology publications and attend the technology trade shows. And they use the latest and greatest Internet and video conferencing technology to communicate with their clients. This agency attracts technology clients because they live and breathe technology.

2 Outmoded services. *What should we stop doing?*

When you're clear about your agency brand, you realize that sometimes there are services or capabilities that you offer but don't really need. Most of the time, these services are only marginal from a profitability standpoint. What's the point of staffing for these services if your target clients don't really need them and they don't contribute much (or anything) to your bottom line?

For example, there's no value in keeping your sales promotion department if you have decided to re-focus your agency brand around corporate communications. In this case, a sales promotion capability is simply a vestige of the past. It becomes more work than it's worth to try and feed it with projects that don't really fit your positioning as an agency. Better to focus on disciplines that support where you're going, not where you've been.

3 Strategic alliances. *For the needed services we don't or can't offer, can we find strategic business partners?*

Agencies wrestle a lot with the question of Internet marketing. When the first rush of dotcom fever hit the business world, many agencies rushed into the interactive business, believing that soon their entire business would be going digital. As things in the Internet space calmed down a bit, agencies came to their senses and realized that many aspects of Web marketing are highly specialized, and require quite a different skill set than most agencies have.

Internet marketing is a good example of an area where agencies (no matter what their positioning) should ask the question, "Should we do this ourselves, or should we find a business partner?" Having the core competency to design a Web site is one thing, but when you get into areas of sophisticated Web site architecture, functionality, and usability, that's another matter. The same goes for e-commerce and customer relationship management (CRM). Do your clients need these things? In many cases, absolutely. But you may serve them best by working with an Internet marketing company that employs designers, developers, and programmers that know this area cold.

A Philadelphia agency gathered their management team in the conference room to consider the question of in-house vs. outsource and came up with this list.

Consumer insights	Internal capability
Strategic planning	Internal capability
Measuring and tracking success	Internal capability
Internet marketing	Find strategic alliance
Direct marketing	Find strategic alliance
Sales training	Find strategic alliance
Customer relationship management	Find strategic alliance
Event planning	Find strategic alliance

Remember, it increases (not decreases) client trust when you tell them you can't do something. If you can't deliver a service with a high standard of excellence, don't do it. But find someone else who can.

4 Proprietary approaches. *Could we develop our own proprietary processes that would add value to our agency brand?*

An agency with a reputation in "natural products" (nutritional supplements, organic foods, natural remedies, etc.) has many interesting opportunities to build their brand. It certainly helps that they're in a particularly hot category with tremendous growth potential, but there's even more they can do to build their agency brand to become more attractive to clients in this category.

For example, what about formulating a proprietary branding process specifically for natural products brands? How about developing a research methodology that helps predict the success of new natural products brands? Or sponsoring an ongoing national survey that tracks trends and new developments in the natural products category?

If you were a manufacturer of natural products, isn't this the kind of agency you would want to hire? When you have a clear picture of what kind of agency you are, there are many things you can do to provide added value to a select group of clients.

5 Client service changes. *Does our positioning suggest changes in the way we service and communicate with our clients?*

If your agency survives on local business only, servicing your clients is a pretty straightforward matter. But if you have an agency focus that attracts clients from around the country (or around the world), client service issues take on new importance. Deciding to make the move from being a local generalist to a national specialist can have far-reaching implications in terms of both staffing and technology.

An agency in the eastern U.S. that specializes in healthcare has no local clients at all. Needless to say, they leverage technology to stay in constant contact with their clients – not just e-mail, but Internet conferencing, ad proofing, large file transfers via a special agency FTP site, and even a dedicated client extranet where the client can view any of this information at will.

Beyond the question of geography, the way your agency is positioned can have other effects on the issue of client service. For one thing, your client service people should be experts not just in advertising and marketing, but also in your chosen area of focus. If you are focused on outdoor recreation, it's only natural that the best account managers would be those who are outdoor enthusiasts themselves. In that case, why not an entire agency of outdoor enthusiasts? Imagine the value that kind of agency would bring to a sporting goods client vs. an agency that just dabbles in it.

THE AGENCY SKILL SET

Besides making ads, agencies can - or rather, should - develop many other aspects of the client's brand. Consider which of the following capabilities you currently have or want to develop as part of your agency's core competencies.

Affiliate marketing
Analyst relations
Annual reports
Association marketing
Beta testing
Brand planning
Brand positioning
Brand equity development
Business development training
Cause-related marketing
Community relations
Corporate communications
Corporate identity
Crisis management
Custom publishing
Customer satisfaction programs
Database design and management
Direct marketing
E-Business strategies
E-Marketing
Employee relations
Employee training
Ethnic marketing
Events
Executive coaching
Fulfillment services
Fundraising
Graphic design
Guerilla marketing
In-store advertising and sales promotion
Interactive services
Internet marketing
Interior design
Investor relations
Labor relations
Lead management
Loyalty marketing

(Continued on next page)

Marketing planning
Media buying
Media planning
Media relations
Media training
Naming programs
New product development
Non-profit marketing
Package design
Political campaign management
Pre/post IPO marketing
Product placement (TV, films & other)
Public affairs
Public relations
Recruitment advertising
Research
Sales support
Sales promotion
Speech writing
Strategic planning
TV program content development
Telemarketing
Trade show production
Trade show support
Viral marketing
Web site design and development

6 **Additional information resources.** *To add to our expertise in our area of focus, do we need access to new or different information resources?*

When you decide to focus your agency, you often need access to specialized information resources you didn't have before. An obvious example is an agency that markets to Latinos. To serve their clients effectively, this kind of agency would certainly need access to all major secondary research about the Hispanic market – demographic trends, buying behavior, purchasing power, etc. This means subscriptions to the national marketing databases that report on the Hispanic population.

Similarly, agencies that focus on technology subscribe to databases that report on competitive spending in the tech category. Business-to-business agencies subscribe to *BtoB* magazine right along with *Advertising Age*. Agencies that market to outdoors enthusiasts subscribe to studies published by the Outdoor Retailers Association.

7 **Industry support.** *Would the support and resources available from membership in industry associations or agency networks help enhance our agency brand?*

An agency in Northern California with a niche in public transportation occupies a prominent place in the American Public Transportation Association. They attend the conferences, speak at the seminars, volunteer on the committees, and serve on the boards. That's pretty smart, since most of their prospective clients belong to APTA as well.

Given the client categories you serve, have you involved your agency in appropriate trade associations? Do you attend the trade shows? Are you recognized as an industry expert?

The success of your agency brand can also be enhanced by memberships in industry associations. And unless you're part of a large multi-office agency, chances are you can also benefit from the networking and information sharing that comes from membership in an agency network.

HOW THE BEST AGENCIES DO IT

Making changes to your services and capabilities to match your positioning is a critical first step on the road to agency branding. While you're at it, engage your management team in some more soul searching and compare your approach in the area of "product" to some of the industry's best practices. What do the best agencies do differently?

THEY ARE BRILLIANT ON THE BASICS

It's sad but true that many agencies are so caught up with questions like how to decorate the lobby or which kind of file servers to buy that they ignore the simple skills and talents that make an agency successful in the first place. It's very much like a successful NBA team. The victor at the end of the season may have cool uniforms, good-looking cheerleaders, and a spanking new arena, but it's a sure bet that this team is also brilliant on the basics; they dribble well, they pass well, and they shoot well.

Scores of agencies have leading-edge décor, hip people, and cool business cards, but they are *not* brilliant on the basics. Their staff is poorly trained, their work is pedestrian, and they have little or no teamwork. They talk the talk, but they don't walk the walk. Jonathan Bond and Richard Kirshenbaum make the same assessment:

Agencies become famous by focusing on what they do best.

"Turn on the television. Why are the ads so bad, you ask? It's because there are very few agencies that are dedicated to doing great work. There are perhaps as few as 40 or 50 agencies in the United States that can actually manufacture a good campaign, and possibly 10 that do it consistently. That is out of 9,200 listed in the Redbook of Advertising Agencies. When a review for a high-profile domestic account comes up, it almost always lands at one of these select firms."[1]

THEY DO WHAT THEY DO BEST AND FIND RESOURCES FOR THE REST

Agencies become famous by focusing on what they do best. My friend Tom Monahan calls this "playing within your game." Tom observes that, "Some of the best athletes in the world are great because they play within their game. Some of the best singers and musicians are great because they don't try to do things they can't do."[2]

The very successful British agency Bartle Bogle Hegarty (famous for its work for international brands like Levis, Hagen-Daas, and Audi), owes a lot of its success to sticking to what it does best. "The trouble with agencies," says agency co-founder John Hegarty, "is they don't limit themselves to what they're good at."[3]

To focus on your core competencies and to avoid dancing around questions about your capabilities, invest some time finding business partners you can trust in areas like these.

Areas of Consideration for Business Partnerships

   Web development and design
   Digital marketing
   Direct marketing
   Database marketing
   On-line public relations
   Sales promotion
   Corporate identity
   Marketing research
   Account planning
   Investor relations
   Media buying

Legal services
National and international affiliates

Ogilvy & Mather took a giant leap in the area of strategic alliances by forging relationships with a network of creative boutiques they call "The Syndicate." This group of independently-owned shops collaborates on creative assignments for major O&M clients and helps develop work for new business presentations.

THEY DON'T JUST SAY THEY INTE-GRATE, THEY REALLY INTEGRATE

If every agency in America is a "full-service, integrated marketing communications firm" (like they say they are), why do clients chronically complain about the lack of integration from their agencies?

Unfortunately, just because agencies have a long list of disciplines doesn't mean they have the discipline to make them all work together. In fact, it's standard operating procedure in most agencies to have individual silos for individual disciplines. The advertising unit and the public relations unit may have shared clients, but they don't have shared goals, shared information, and shared methods of working together. The agency is a bit like Frankenstein — made up of different unrelated parts.

DELIVERING ON THE PROMISE OF INTEGRATION

How can agencies get past their good intentions and actually deliver on their promise of integration?

1. **Implement a cross-training program.** This is an obvious first step to achieving better agency integration, yet agencies seldom take the initiative to do it. Simply put, the idea is to schedule sessions in which one department teaches another.
2. **Hold monthly integration meetings by account.** During interdisciplinary meetings, have a representative of each discipline discuss the current actions items in their area of responsibility. Consider drafting a master status report for the client to show how the agency is working together to achieve consistent messaging.
3. **Make integration the focus of your agency's intranet.** What better place to create an integrated environment that on your agency's intranet? Here you can put all relevant client information, accessible by all members of the account team. With an intranet, everyone from the advertising account coordinator to the head of the direct response division can view shared information on an account.
4. **Share the work of all departments.** It's ironic that so much of the actual work produced by the agency goes virtually unseen by everyone except the people who produced it. How can the agency build a consistent, synergistic brand identity for a client if the work isn't shared with all members of the team?
5. **Decide which disciplines are "portal disciplines" through which accounts will be administered.** When you have an "integrated client," think carefully about which discipline should take the lead in the relationship. It doesn't have to be the advertising team, but it does have to be

(Continued on next page)

formally assigned. Remember, if everyone is responsible, no one is responsible.

6. **Establish a dedicated war room for integrated clients.** If you can spare the space, dedicate an entire room to displaying work, plans, reports, and ideas for major integrated clients. It's also the best possible place to hold a client meeting – with or without the client.

7. **Appoint a director of brand integration to make sure integration is happening in the agency as a whole.** If your agency is a particularly difficult case, maybe what you need is an "integration czar" – a senior person in the agency whose job it is to remind and encourage members of all disciplines to talk, meet, and communicate about a client's business. This is not an easy job, and it will take someone who has earned the trust and respect of others in the agency.

8. **Implement a cross-training program.** If the left hand doesn't know what the right hand is doing, a cross-department training program can really help. It's not so surprising that advertising people don't really understand what PR people do, and vice-versa; they're very different disciplines. Some agencies require their employees (particularly their new employees) to complete a core curriculum in interdepartmental training.

It all starts by adopting the attitude "Many disciplines, one team." (Try posting this thought in a conspicuous place in the agency.) Integration is possible, but it doesn't happen naturally.

THEY HAVE TURNED THE ENTIRE AGENCY INTO THE CREATIVE DEPARTMENT

Virtually all agencies claim to have great creative work. Only a handful really do. What's the difference? The talent of the creative director? Sometimes, but not always.

Some agencies with a lackluster creative product simply aren't organized to produce great work. Often, heavy-handed agency managers second-guess the work and opinions of the creative director. Account management people are not taught to recognize, present, and defend great work. And counterproductive systems and procedures stifle creative thinking with too much paperwork and not enough face-to-face communication.

Maybe you do need a new six-figure creative director from San Francisco. But sometimes you can make dramatic improvements by simply removing the obstacles that stand in the way of great work. Chances are, the talent is already there.

You can, in fact, turn the entire agency into the creative department by underscoring the value and importance of creativity in *everything* you do. You can start by screening all new employees (not just creatives) in part for their creative judgment. You can encourage other disciplines (not just creatives) to develop portfolios of their best work. You can ask all employees (not just creatives) to review their most creative accomplishments in their performance review.

More ideas? Show the work of other departments (not just the creative department) at agency staff meetings. Give a monthly award for creative problem solving (instead of the usual "employee of the month."). Get a subscription to *Communication Arts* for everyone in the agency. Start a creativity reading program. Creativity is, after all, what an agency ultimately has to sell.

THEY HAVE AN EXTREMELY INTERACTIVE WAY OF WORKING TOGETHER

How many times have you heard, "I'm the copywriter, so don't mess with my copy. I'm the art director, so don't mess with my layout. I'm the account executive, so don't mess with my strategy." It's part of the big wall that can divide one discipline from another if we're not careful. The movement toward "agency teams" has helped break down this cat-and-dog dynamic, but it needs to go further than that.

Lee Clow of TBWA/Chiat Day raises a very thought-provoking question. He wonders, if we agree that the consumer decision making process is complex and emotional, why is the process we use to develop our messages to consumers so structured and rational?[4]

Agencies need to replace "meetings" with a more interactive way of working together.

In other words, crafting a message that will speak meaningfully to the complex animal we call a consumer isn't just a matter of the account manager opening the job, the copywriter writing the copy, the art director doing the layout, traffic putting the comp on the account manager's desk at 2:45, and the account manager walking out the door at 3:00 to present it to the client. Yet, sadly enough, that's how it works a lot of the time in a lot of agencies.

The process agencies use to develop marketing solutions needs to be much, much more interactive between departments. It needs to be more open, inclusive, and trusting. For one thing, this means replacing "meetings" with a more productive way of working together. It means finding a way to get everyone excited about contributing.

Lowe in New York has a long corridor they call "The Wall," where every member of the creative department has nameplates under which they pin up ads they did recently. At any given point, there are about 300 pieces of work on display for all to see.

MEASURES OF SUCCESS

Agency executives would rightly argue that advertising and marketing can't possibly take responsibility for the basic measures of business success (profit margin, return on assets, growth, etc.). That's fair enough, but there are some basic things agencies can help measure and track for their clients:

Brand Awareness
Unaided awareness of the brand
Aided awareness of the brand

Brand Benefits
How the brand compares to the "ideal" product attributes in the category

Brand Quality
Perceived quality of the brand vs. other brands

Brand Preference
Which brands in the category are preferred and why

Brand Usage
How often the brand is purchased
Intent to purchase our brand vs. other brands

Brand Loyalty
Exclusive use of the brand (vs. other brands)

Brand Touch Points
Extent to which the brand is perceived consistently in all communications

Sales
Dollars
Units
Customer count
By product or service

Market Share
By category
By product or service
Geographically

"This means everybody gets to see what everybody else is working on," says Lowe's Gary Goldsmith. "I like to have people talking, even arguing about all the agency's work, and this provokes that."[5] Interaction is as important in agencies as it is in sports. Can you imagine a football game in which the game begins with a briefing by the coach, but then the team never huddles one single time during the entire game? The quarterback does his best, the receivers do their best, the nose tackles do their best, but they never stop to huddle, talk about the game, and make changes to the game plan. But that's what we agencies do all the time, day after day. We have a creative brief, but no briefing. Concepts, but no concept review meeting. We don't stop often enough to huddle.

The Martin Agency talks about "swirling" — a word for quick informal meetings to continually improve work as it moves through the agency. You can call it "scrumming" if you prefer a rugby analogy, or even "huddling." A leading business-to-business agency, RiechesBaird, calls it "storming."

R&R Partners calls their process "swarming," and its used by everybody in the agency from account people to creatives. While the whole point of "swarming" is to keep things loose and open, swarming does have some important guidelines.[6]

Swarming Guidelines

1. Anyone can call a swarm.
2. A swarm can happen anywhere.
3. A swarm is informal.
4. A swarm can be spontaneous.
5. Not everybody has to be available to attend a swarm (they can catch up later).
6. A swarm is not a traffic meeting.
7. In a swarm, anyone can have a good idea.

Call the process whatever you like, but agencies need to break down the walls and the linear way they have of moving a job through the agency.

THEY KNOW THAT THEY SERVE THEIR CLIENTS BEST BY GIVING THEM GREAT WORK

Agency managers know that the pressure to turn out faster, cheaper work grows with each new client and every passing year. You could, if you really wanted, position your agency as one that does work faster and cheaper than other agencies. "The Ad Store" is just such a concept. Just be aware that "fast and cheap" is a dangerous game, and one that is particularly difficult for a professional services company. As David Ogilvy was fond of saying, "Any damn fool can put on a deal, but it takes genius, faith, and perseverance to build a brand."[7]

The advertising agency lives at the intersection of art and commerce. Advertising is a business, but it's also an art. And clients have been pushing artists for "faster and cheaper" ever since the Pope complained to Michelangelo about the time and cost overruns on the Sistine Chapel. But if you think about it, every major success story in our business is one of quality, not quantity. There's no question that business cycles are shorter and demands for financial results are stronger. New technology allows agencies to perform in seconds what used to take hours. So the truth is that agencies *can* produce work faster (and perhaps cheaper). The question is whether or not they *should*.

THEY DON'T JUST CREATE GREAT WORK, THEY ACTUALLY GET IT PRODUCED

America is populated with hundreds of agencies that produce thousands of outstanding creative concepts. The creative directors at most of these shops have a morgue of rejected ideas on the floors of their offices. They think of their clients as "the place where great ideas go to die."

But the real difference between a good agency and a great agency is that the great agency actually gets their concepts *produced*. As creative coach Tom Monahan says, "I believe that an idea is not great if it doesn't ultimately see the light of day. That, to me, is like hitting a home run in batting practice. It doesn't count for anything. The real superstars in baseball are the players who do it in prime time, just as the real winners in any other industry are the people who have new ideas that actually become reality."[8]

How do the great agencies do it? For starters, they don't just show up to a client meeting with a stack of black boards under their arm. They agonize over how the work should be presented, and they rehearse who's going to say what well in advance of a client meeting. Then they don't just spread a variety of ideas on the client's conference table; they carefully lead up to an agency recommendation.

Contrast this with the way it works at most agencies, where the account team piles in the car, already late for the client meeting. The account executive frantically flips through the concepts, seeing them for the first time. The team shows up at the client without a rehearsal, without an agreed-upon point of view, and without a clear agency recommendation. In situations like these, it's no wonder that the weakest ideas sometimes emerge as the winners.

Another principle practiced by successful creative shops is to improve the result at the *back end* (the produced work) by improving the process at the *front end*. It's often said in agencies that "There's never enough time to do it right the first time, but there always enough time to do it over." In hundreds of interviews with creative people over the years, the most common response to the question of how the agency can improve its creative work is almost always the same: "Give us not only more time, but better information." The best creative directors simply put their foot down and say "No creative brief, no concepts."

THEY DON'T "SELL" THEIR WORK OR SERVICES, THEY JUST BUILD TRUST

Why do companies hire professional service firms? For outside expertise, counsel and advice. Of course clients need ads, brochures, annual reports, and Web sites, but they could probably do a lot of that in-house if they really wanted to. What they ultimately seek is an objective, third-party point of view.

When clients perceive that you are trying to "sell" them something – a bigger media buy, a new corporate identity program that they don't really need, etc. – it erodes the currency that has the most value for agencies: trust. The most successful agencies don't really sell their products and services at all. They just do the right thing for their clients, whether it benefits the agency or not. My friend Luc Geelen who runs an agency in Belgium lives by the axiom, "Look after the advertising and the money will look after itself."[9]

The principals of a notable agency in the Mountain West routinely help their clients navigate through such troubled waters as union strikes, rate hikes, and other crisis communications situations, usually without charging an additional fee. Perhaps that's one reason many of their client relationships date back ten (and in some cases twenty) years or more.

THEY CLARIFY CLIENT EXPECTATIONS EVERY STEP OF THE WAY

It's true that most clients want an objective outside point of view from their agency. But not until their agency has bothered to take the time to first understand the client's expectations. Deep down inside, the thing that clients value most is an agency that *listens*. Not an agency that just takes orders or is afraid to say no. But an agency that is willing to make the effort to understand what the client really wants and needs from the relationship.

Most of us are pretty reluctant to take a doctor's prescribed cure (like major surgery) unless we know the doctor has taken the time to make a good diagnosis. Good agencies, like good doctors, listen first and dispense advice later.

Agencies can make dramatic improvements by simply removing the obstacles to great work.

THE BRAND REVIEW

One of the best ways to make sure you're serving clients effectively is to gather your best minds together for a "brand review," in which you take a big-picture view of the client's business and think about other ways you can help. A good brand review includes a look at things like:

1. Status of the industry and current trends
2. Current client issues and concerns
3. Competitive review, including competitive creative work
4. Market segments and target audiences
5. Client sales history and marketing successes
6. Current brand awareness and attitudes
7. Share of mind and share of market
8. Spending history and projections
9. Consumer understanding and recent research findings
10. Current branding strategy
11. Current work (from all disciplines, not just advertising)
12. Results, past and current
13. Opportunities for delivering added value and proactive service

Once while attending an agency seminar, I was struck by a comment made by a wise creative director who said, "After years of frustration getting work approved by young, inexperienced marketing directors who don't know what they're doing, I've finally found the answer. It's disarmingly simple," he said, "but it's the only thing that really works. Empathy. Empathize so completely with the client and her problems and concerns that she finally understands that you're out to help her, not 'sell' her."

It's been said that Bill Bernbach used to carry around a little slip of paper in his jacket that said, "Remember, the client might be right." Judging from the quality of work he produced over the years, this philosophy served him well.

It helps to get new client relationships off on the right foot. Unfortunately, most clients and their agencies are in such a hurry to get started on hot projects that they neglect to take the time to spend a few hours discussing what each party expects from the relationship. The 90 minutes it takes up front to clarify mutual expectations will save you hours – if not days or weeks – of grief later on.

Kirshenbaum, Bond & Partners begins new relationships with what they call a Contract of Expectations. "Before we being working with clients we always agree upfront on how we're going to work together and how we will resolve conflict," they say. "We talk about the hot buttons – situations that developed from past agency-client relationships that would provoke dissatisfaction if they were repeated."

"Seek first to understand, then to be understood," advises Stephen Covey in his landmark book, *The 7 Habits of Highly Successful People.* Covey believes that most people do not listen with the intent to understand; they listen with the intent to reply. They're either speaking or preparing to speak.[10] Dare to be one of the agencies that sublimates its ego and really listens before it recommends.

THEY AREN'T AFRAID TO GIVE ALL MEMBERS OF THE TEAM DIRECT CONTACT WITH THE CLIENT

Why do writers, art directors, and media planners get upset when the account manager returns from a client meeting with a briefcase full of changes? A big part of the reason is that these other team members really don't know (hence, respect) the client. As long as the account manager is the sole ambassador of the agency – carrying work back and forth in a big black bag – other members of the team will have little empathy for what the client wants to do differently and why.

Forward-thinking agencies give all members of the team contact with the client. Creatives present creative work, media planners present media work, account planners present research work, and so on. When the client has feedback, comments, or changes, these same team members are there to hear it firsthand. This accomplishes two important things. First, it helps calm the traditional cat-and-dog relationship between account people and other departments, because the account person no longer is always the bearer of bad tidings (the other team members hear the criticism directly from the source). Second, it improves the relationship between the other departments and the client, because they actually get to know one another as living, breathing human beings.

Agencies with "dedicated teams" work this way. Why shouldn't every agency?

THEY INVOLVE THE CLIENT MORE (NOT LESS) THAN OTHER AGENCIES

After weeks of late nights and Chinese take-out, the creative team is finally ready to present their recommendations for next year's campaign. Their enthusiasm turns to disappointment when the client approves the weakest idea of the bunch instead of the strongest. Should they have presented with more conviction? Defended with more courage?

Very often, the best ideas are lost because the client was involved only at the end of the process – not the beginning. Clients aren't given an opportunity to feel ownership in an idea. Instead, they are kept at a safe distance from the rogue creative minds of the agency. They are barred from seeing the rough ideas pinned up in the agency's inner sanctum, and instead are shown highly polished concepts in the sterile environment of a conference room. They have no idea how the agency got from point A to point B, and they have little appreciation for all the ideas that were considered but discarded.

Why? Because they weren't there. They weren't involved. They weren't asked for their opinion, their perspective, or their feedback until the whole process was over. Is it any wonder that clients feel a lack of partnership with their agencies?

THEY KNOW THAT CLIENTS DON'T NEED MORE INFORMATION, THEY NEED MORE INSIGHT

The best client organizations are obsessed with their customer. They want not just customers, but "raving fans," so they study customer buying habits, customer purchase patterns and customer loyalty. Just the same, because clients are so close to their own business, sometimes it's difficult for them to see their customers from an objective point of view. They're in the middle of the forest and need someone to help them see all the trees.

Bill Bernbach believed that, "At the heart of an effective creative philosophy is the belief that nothing is so powerful as an insight into human nature, what compulsions drive a man, what instincts dominate his action, *even though his language so often camouflages what really motivates him.*"[11] He didn't know it, but he was speaking of the discipline of account planning.

If you're lucky enough to have account planning in your agency, then you're already light years ahead in your ability to help your clients truly understand their customers. Unfortunately, the discipline of account planning is still quite misunderstood. A lot of agencies say they have account planning without really even knowing what it is.

Adweek once took a stab at trying to visually illustrate what an account planner is, and it turned out to be a pretty strange looking beast. That's because good planners are part anthropologist, part sociologist, part strategist, part researcher, and part writer; but good planners can make a huge difference in the kind of work the agency puts out.

A few years ago, a well-known West Coast shop presented a new campaign to its computer gaming client. Their presentation went something like this: "We're quite certain you're not going to like the work we're about to show you. We don't even like it all that much ourselves. But according to the extensive account planning research we've done, your audience – 12 year-old kids — will *love* it." The campaign was approved with no changes.

Of course, one of the biggest benefits of account planning is that clients generally support work that's rooted in a deep understanding of the consumer. But if you're just guessing, it's back to the agency's opinion vs. the client's opinion. And you know how that goes. Account planning helps reduce the gamble.

Can you run a successful agency without account planning? Probably. Is it a panacea for better advertising? Not always. "Planning is very far from perfect," says account planner John Webster. "But like democracy, it's far better than the alternatives."[12] And to bring account planning into a bottom line perspective, Jean-Marie Dru, head of the global BDDP Group believes "We will always make more money by doing a good job of account planning than by trying to save on office space and personnel expenses."[13]

Remember, clients already have enough information. They just don't have enough insight.

THEY PRACTICE FIRE PREVENTION RATHER THAN FIRE FIGHTING

All agencies strive to provide responsive client service. There's nothing wrong with this objective, except that clients can get *responsive* service from any agency down the street. A great agency provides *proactive* service. Ask practically any client why they're switching agencies and what do they say? "Because the agency never gave us anything that we didn't ask for." In other words, they were never proactive.

There are always reasons why we're not as proactive as we should be; we're too busy, too distracted, or too unhappy with the number of rush jobs to make the effort to provide the client ideas without being asked.

Great agencies act. Average agencies are acted upon.

This is a serious, chronic problem among agencies. How do you break the cycle and make proactive service happen? One agency I know does it with what they call "Blue Sky Meetings." At an appointed time, the key members of the agency team get together, bring in pizza, and think big-picture about a client's business. After an hour on the white board, they're ready to give their client a whole list of ideas the client never asked for. Unless agencies adopt a formal process like this, procrastination will get the better of us every time.

As a professional services organization, we're paid largely to be proactive. And in the end, we can either act or be acted upon. We can pick up the phone and recommend a promotional idea to help stem the tide of declining sales, or we can wait for the client to call and ask us to develop a promotional idea to help stem the tide of declining sales. Act or react. If you were a client, which kind of agency would you prefer?

THEY GEAR EVERYTHING AROUND THE CLIENT'S SUCCESS, NOT THE AGENCY'S

Clients want agencies to feel more accountable for results. Surprisingly, many agencies do a poor (or nonexistent) job of helping the client track results. That's because they really don't fully understand what constitutes success in the first place.

All client companies have basic measures of business success, but this is a language that a lot of agency executives don't really speak. In *What the CEO Wants You to Know*, Ram Charan argues that understanding the basic building blocks of business success will make you infinitely more valuable to a company, no matter what your role. "The most successful business leaders never lose sight of the basics," he asserts. "Their intense focus on the fundamentals of business is, in fact, the secret to their success…they have a keen sense of how a business makes money."[14]

The debate over accountability is raging strong on both sides of the fence. Agencies desperately want to be strategic business partners with their clients, but feel their clients often just treat them like a pair of hands. "Partnership" may in fact be the most popular word in agency self-promotion literature.

So why don't more clients let their agencies into the inner circle of business decision-making? Why do clients continue to treat their agencies more like suppliers than counselors? Because clients don't believe their agencies are very accountable for results. And to them, that's the definition of partnership. A partner is vested in the success of the enterprise. Most agencies just make ads, release them to the media, and move onto the next project.

More importantly, agencies typically don't suffer any consequences from a poorly performing campaign (other than they might eventually lose the account). Sometimes while the client is losing sales, the agency is winning awards. If you were a client, you might feel there's something wrong with that equation.

HOW A BRAND COMMUNICATIONS FIRM IS DIFFERENT FROM AN "AD AGENCY"

1. It identifies and prioritizes all key audiences of the brand (not just consumers).
2. It identifies and prioritizes all key points of contact with the brand (not just advertising).
3. It monitors and evaluates all brand messages (not just paid messages).
4. It monitors the customer's actual experience purchasing and using the brand (not just what they think about the brand).
5. It considers everything as "media" for their client's message (not just traditional advertising media).
6. It has a system for measuring the quality of brand relationships (not just brand awareness and preference).

"Vendor vs. partner" is a complex and vital issue. But the first step in becoming more of a partner is undoubtedly to take more responsibility for the results your client considers important. This means more than traditional tracking studies. Agencies need to develop an inventory of the "top measures of success" for each major client, then keep an eye on these metrics on a regular basis.

THEY DON'T MANAGE ACCOUNTS, THEY MANAGE BRANDS

It's time for agencies to face the fact that the title "account manager" is much more appropriate for a stock brokerage or insurance agency (where they actually manage "accounts") than it is for an advertising agency. Agencies shouldn't manage accounts. They should manage *brands*.

"Brand manager" is a much better way to refer to people involved in the discipline of client service. The difference can be much more than just titular, however. While the common "account executive" is often more of a project manager, the brand manager is a strategic-minded guardian of the brand.

True, brand managers shouldn't just look after the advertising, they should help oversee *all the points of contact the customer has with the brand*, including:

- How the brand is positioned
- How the brand is packaged or presented
- How the brand is displayed (physical or virtual)
- How the brand is advertised and promoted
- The customer's physical experience with the brand
- How fulfillment is handled
- How sales people interact with customers
- What the sales literature looks like
- How the company answers the phone

Today's brand managers need a deep understanding of the client's business. They need a thorough understanding of the branding process. And they need a working knowledge of all of the major marketing communications disciplines, not just advertising. They need to be able to develop clear, insightful creative briefs. And they should be able to put it all together in a living, breathing marketing communications plan.

Is this the same kind of beast that we used to call the account executive? Perhaps. But consider that forward-thinking agencies are realizing that this skill set is quite different from the administratively talented account executives of the past.

That's why some agencies have actually split the traditional account management function into two jobs; one called something like "brand strategist," and the other "brand manager." Each has a different set of responsibilities:

Brand Strategist	**Brand Manager**
Direction	Execution
The *What*	The *How*

An agency that can provide brand leadership – not just account management – is both a valuable proposition and a rare commodity. And if clients are slow to get on this train, most agencies haven't even packed their bags. A lot of the half-hearted attempts made by agencies to provide 360-degree brand management are more focused on selling agency disciplines than making a concerted effort to communicate with all of the brand's important audiences. As Duncan and Moriarty quip in *Driving Brand Value,* "They have been more interested in creating one invoice than one voice."[15]

My former associate Dave Boede created an agency that successfully weathered economic downturns by addressing areas in ways clients don't typically expect from an ad agency. Says Dave:

> "How many agencies will walk in and say let's look at everything from your sales database to your web site to your call center to your communications programs, making sure we have a closed loop analysis from lead generation to sale? How does that information track? How does that evolve into brand loyalty programs and up-sell opportunities? There is a lack of process in how companies manage and track their sales/marketing systems. This is a unique opportunity for us."[16]

No matter how you're positioned as an agency, you have the opportunity to think beyond traditional audiences and traditional media. You have the opportunity to help your client manage every important point of contact with the brand.

THE AGENCY/CLIENT PERFORMANCE PLAN

For a major bank (not really "First National Bank," as used in this example), an agency in a mid-sized city developed this performance plan after three years of experience with this client.

Evaluation of Past Period

Based on written feedback from First National Bank, the perception of the agency's performance over the past year could be characterized as follows:

Areas of Strength

1. Experience and depth of agency team
2. Strategic input and marketing counsel
3. Anticipating needs without waiting to be asked
4. Client service (responsiveness, contact, timeliness, etc.)
5. Innovative creative work
6. Working relationship
7. Enthusiasm and commitment

Areas for Improvement

1. Knowledge of client's business
2. Cost consciousness
3. Keeping within budgets
4. Listening to and understanding client concerns
5. Willingness to accept client's position

(Continued on next page)

Performance Objectives

Client management at First National Bank would like to see Smith & Jones work to improve the following:

1. Increase the agency's interaction with client contact initiating the assignment.
2. Improve the agency's timeliness in the production of the creative product.
3. Generally show more sensitivity to costs and budgets and exercise more and better cost controls where possible.
4. Continue to improve agency knowledge of the banking industry and First National Bank in particular in order to provide sound advice to grow First National Bank's business.
5. Hold debriefing meetings to discuss and assess results for all major marketing campaigns.

Additionally, Smith & Jones has identified the following areas where First National Bank could contribute to the success of the relationship.

1. Longer lead times and more advance planning for projects.
2. Improve information and input at the beginning of a project.
3. Work together to find a better way to provide for the needs of all divisions and departments of the corporation in a timely manner.
4. Consider the services of Smith & Jones more often in the development of retail merchandising programs.
5. Give the discipline of account planning and its accompanying unorthodox research methods more of a chance to help provide insight into customer wants, needs, and behavior.

Action Plan

1. Schedule periodic attendance at banking industry seminars/trade shows as a means of expanding the working knowledge of the agency.
2. Develop recommended ideas for controlling costs and present in writing to client.
3. Schedule a regular series of "listening" lunches with key First National Bank management in order to better assess and understand client concerns, goals, and objectives.
4. Meet in person with selected branch managers to better understand their viewpoints and needs.

Needed Resources

To help in the accomplishment of the above desired results, the agency asks that First National Bank be willing to:

1. Share results of all major marketing programs on a regular basis. The agency will in turn prepare regular post-campaign analyses for review with the client.
2. In partnership with the marketing department, allow the agency more opportunities to present creative recommendations directly to the person or department for whom the work was created.
3. Provide the agency more consistently with the results of in-house research efforts and invite the agency to attend focus group sessions.
4. Increase agency involvement in planning major marketing programs, including decisions about budgets, possible media, and campaign timing.

(Continued on next page)

Accountability for Results

Results and progress of this agreement will be measured as followed:

1. Periodic meetings between Agency and Client management in order to review the status and effectiveness of the Agency's strategic marketing, advertising, and research recommendations.
2. Agency will solicit written feedback again from Client one year from now.

What changes do you need to make in the way you select, train, and manage your people to help bring your positioning to life?

6 PEOPLE: Building On Natural Talents

IT'S COMMON TO hear advertising described as a people business. In a very real sense, your inventory goes up and down in the elevator every night. In a professional service business, your people are quite literally the face of the agency brand. So to put your best foot forward in the area of "people," consider the following areas.

1 Current staffing.
Do we have the kind of people we need to execute on our positioning?

Needless to say, the most important element in executing your positioning is having the right people with the right talents in the right jobs. This doesn't just mean having good people. It means having people whose knowledge, skills, and talents match the focus of the agency. A database marketing expert is exactly what you need in a direct marketing agency, but wouldn't necessarily be of much help in a firm that has positioned itself as a brand consultancy.

If you have a clear branding strategy for your agency, you can establish clear standards for the kind of employees you need. For example, an agency that transformed from a provider of collateral materials to a full scale business-to-business shop found that many of their employees were skilled in design and production, but didn't have the skill set to provide more strategically-oriented added-value services for its clients. The leaders of this agency defined the qualities that would best support the agency positioning and set new standards for recruitment and employee selection. They also made the difficult but necessary decision to replace several employees who simply didn't fit with the agency brand.

Repositioning your agency can sometimes result in substantially restaffing your agency as well.

2 Roles and responsibilities. *Should roles and responsibilities be redefined to bring the organization into better alignment with our positioning?*

You probably already have a lot of the right people, but they may need different roles or responsibilities. For example, if your agency positioning means that you need to do more work on the Internet, talented art directors working on traditional media solutions need to spend more time designing for the Web. Media planners and buyers have to get deeper into the world of Internet media planning and placement. And client service people need to know more about Internet marketing.

If your people don't understand your positioning, your brand will just be an empty promise

It's possible that your positioning indicates a complete agency reorganization, with new departments, new department heads, and new roles and responsibilities for the partners. At the very least, positioning the agency provides an opportunity to evaluate the contributions of your people and make staffing adjustments accordingly. Make a list of all of your employees, and sort them into one of these four groups:

Critical to our success and positioning
Important contributors to our success and positioning
Marginal contributors to our success and positioning
Detrimental to our success and positioning

Employees who fall into the first two categories are keepers. Those whom you view as marginal should either be redirected into new roles where they can become more important contributors, or help them move on to another job. And for those who actually have a detrimental effect on the agency, you have no choice but to help them find employment elsewhere.

Terminating an employee is difficult business. But when you have underperforming people, you are doing both the agency and the employee a disservice by keeping them on board. There are plenty of good reasons why continued employment is bad for both parties:

- The underperforming employee has a negative effect on those around him. Other employees are usually the first to see that this person can't or won't do the job that needs to be done.
- The underperforming employee contributes little to the success of the agency, and in some cases may even be disadvantageous.
- The underperforming employee is likely unhappy himself, because he's in a role that is not well suited to his strengths. He would actually feel more fulfilled and contented elsewhere.

There is usually only one reason *not* to terminate him – the agency manager finds the process too distasteful. Just consider that you will probably be helping – not hurting – the miscast employee by helping him move onto something where he can be more productive. And you'll most certainly be helping your agency.

3 Hiring standards. *Given our focus, what kind of criteria should we use when selecting new employees?*

Most agencies recruit for experience (deduced from the resume) and attitude (discerned from the interview), but recruiting to match your positioning requires that you hire and staff based on three key criteria:

Comprehension. Does this person possess enough knowledge about the job and the business? *Will this knowledge help us deliver on our positioning?*

Competencies. Does this person have the skills and abilities to do the job? *Are these abilities what the agency needs to deliver on its positioning?*

Character. Does this person's character, attitude and personality fit the culture of the company? *Will theses character traits help us deliver on our positioning?*

Recruiting the right people is an art, but there's also some science to it — something most agencies tend to overlook. No one should ever be hired just on the basis of a resume and an interview. It's too easy for the applicant to make the resume and interview look good. This incomplete approach routinely results in the wrong people in the wrong jobs. The hiring mistakes in some agencies are legendary.

While you may never achieve a perfect track record of hiring great people, you can dramatically improve the odds of finding a good fit by using one of the many assessment tools on the market. Don't make the mistake of thinking you can assess character (personality, attitude, and work habits) from an interview. You can't get this information by asking point blank questions. You need to use a validated assessment tool, many of which are available for use online.

4 Professional development. *What can we do to educate our people about the agency brand and train them to continually improve their performance?*

Living the brand involves people, not just things. If your people don't understand your positioning, your brand will just be an empty promise — no matter what you say on your Web site. Agencies that have succeeded in establishing a brand take absolutely every opportunity to educate and motivate their staff about the agency brand.

The first step is a session in which you teach your employees:

Our purpose. The rallying cry that gives meaning to our business lives. Our holy crusade. The difference we are trying to make in the world.

Our principles. The things that we will always do and the things we will never do. The things we value most and won't compromise. The lines we draw in the sand.

Our positioning. The way we differentiate ourselves from the other thousands of agencies in America. Why every company in the U.S. is *not* a prospective client. Why the prospective clients we do want would fly across the country to do business with us.

For your purpose, principles, and positioning to make a real difference in the way you do business, they must be understood at a deep level throughout the entire organization. I know of one agency principal that walks up and down the halls giving on-the-spot bonuses for employees who can articulate what the agency stands for.

If employees truly understand the agency's purpose, principles, and positioning, the best of them will intuitively understand what they need to do as individuals to support the agency brand. Just the same, an ongoing professional development program would make a huge difference — not only in the fulfillment of the brand, but the fulfillment of the individual employee.

Sadly, professional development has all but disappeared from the agency scene. Long gone are the days when agencies would put budding young assistant account executives through a six-month course before they could legitimately claim the title "Account Executive."

The disappearance of training is not just a matter of economics. Agencies stopped their training programs in the go-go years of the 1990s. It's a cultural shift that has contrib-

THE ESSENTIAL AGENCY TRAINING PROGRAM

Starting and sustaining a professional development program requires a commitment most agencies aren't willing to make. If you'd like to be one of the exceptions, here's a good place to start:

Product
Becoming an expert on your client's business
Providing first-class client service
Developing inspiring creative briefs
Making the most of media
Developing better creative judgment
Working with account planning
Growing current clients
Presenting agency work and recommendations
Measuring success

People
Making the best use of your time
Becoming an agency leader
Managing agency resources
Managing people

Process
Organizing for success
Managing the financial side of the business

Promotion
Marketing the agency
Achieving success in new business

Place
Making effective use of technology

uted to the trend agencies have been lamenting the most: the loss of client confidence in agency people as experts and trusted advisors.

Rob White of Fallon may have actually underestimated the rate of change in the advertising business when he said "Every 18 months, what we don't know about our business doubles, and the time to learn it halves."[1] Which makes the current lack of training in agencies an even more desperate situation.

Professional development is such a perennial problem that industry organizations like the American Association of Advertising Agencies have concluded that since agencies can't or won't do it for themselves, solutions like on-line training need to be explored. But does training have to be such a mind-numbing challenge? Is it really that difficult to give your employees opportunities to sharpen their skills?

Training can actually be accomplished in a number of different ways:

Inside training consisting of in-service courses by department or function, provided by qualified on-staff instructors. These internal sessions can also be taught by professionals from outside the agency.

Outside training consisting of seminars and conferences hosted by industry associations, consulting firms, or other providers.

Formal training provided by colleges, universities, or other institutions of higher learning. Many of these classes may provide credits leading to an advanced degree.

Agency staffers can't sharpen their skills or align their skills behind the brand unless you provide the opportunities. Training shouldn't be one of those things that you'll get to when you have the time, because you never will have the time. You just have to get to it anyway.

5 New employee orientation. *Are we taking the opportunity to indoctrinate new employees about our purpose, principles, and positioning?*

At the end of their first day of work, most agency employees are armed with a desk, a computer, and a network password – but no formal introduction to the agency. At the end of their first week, they're still lacking a basic familiarization with the agency organization, systems, or culture. At the end of their second week, a lot of new employees have concluded that they will pretty much have to figure these things out by themselves.

Contrast this with the agencies that take new employee orientation seriously. What better opportunity to align your people with your positioning than teaching new hires about the agency brand?

Use an employee's first day to orient, not to work. The first day creates the first impression. Talk up the agency brand up front, and your people will know you're serious about it.

When you think about it, your people are actually the most prominent manifestation of your brand. The former steward of one of the most well-branded companies in the world – Nike – argues that your brand is defined "by the accomplishments of your best employee – the shining star of the company who can do no wrong – as well as by the mishaps of the worst hire that you ever made."[2]

6 **Performance reviews.** *How can we improve our performance review process and use it to help reinforce the agency brand?*

THE EFFECTIVE NEW EMPLOYEE ORIENTATION

Resist the temptation to throw new employees into the fire on their first day. Much better to give them a thorough tour of the firehouse first.

Purpose
Agency purpose (beyond making money)

Principles
Agency principles (the things we will always do and the things we'll never do)

Positioning
Agency positioning (who we are, what we are, what we do, who we do it for)

Product
Specific job functions and assignments
Strategic planning approach
Creative philosophy

People
Agency organization
Employee benefits
Agency policies and employee manual
Performance review system
Training program

Process
Job processing system
Time sheets
Agency reports (status, conference, etc.)
Agency filing systems
Estimating and billing systems
Production and media systems
Client compensation systems

Promotion
Agency self-promotion materials
Agency publicity, awards and recognition
Target prospects and new business approach

Place
Office furniture, supplies and equipment
Phone and voice mail system
E-mail system and policies
Computer systems and network
Building security and emergency procedures
Administrative assistance

THE STRENGTHS-BASED PERFORMANCE REVIEW

To focus performance reviews on employee strengths instead of weaknesses, ask employees to drive the process themselves by answering the following questions.

1. **Key responsibilities.** How would you describe your major roles and responsibilities at the agency?
2. **Key areas of strength.** What natural talents do you bring to your job? (Not knowledge you have acquired or skills you have learned, but innate strengths.)*
3. **Key contributions.** What have been your biggest contributions to the agency this past year? Since you've been with the company?
4. **Key outcomes for the company.** By leveraging your natural strengths, what are the biggest contributions you can make to the success of the agency and its clients in the coming year?
5. **Key outcomes for you.** What are some of your own goals and aspirations for the future? What objectives do you have for your own personal development?
6. **Needed support and resources.** What additional help, training, authority, or resources do you need to accomplish your key outcomes? What can your supervisor do to help neutralize your fundamental weaknesses* so you can continue to build on your fundamental strengths?

Every one of us has strengths and weaknesses. Weaknesses that can be addressed by learning or practicing should be addressed immediately. Weaknesses that are as inherent as our natural strengths are a different matter. Instead of trying to change what probably can't be changed, can your role or responsibilities be modified so you can do what you do best?

Because your positioning is based on your agency's strengths – not your weaknesses – you should consider applying the same logic to evaluating your people. It's what your employees do *well* that adds value to the organization. Strengths contribute everything, weaknesses contribute nothing. So focus on developing people's strong points, and try to make their weak points immaterial.

Consider how focusing on strengths can change the tone of the dreaded "performance review." The reason supervisors and employees alike have a distaste for performance reviews is because they are based on job descriptions that make perfect performance virtually impossible. Not only do agency staffers vary widely in God-given abilities like attention to detail and interpersonal communication skills, they would have to be superhuman to score a "10" on things like "demonstrates a complete understanding of all facets of a client's business." (We all know nobody is *that* good.) Rather than rating employees on mundane qualities like office cleanliness, focus on what the employee can contribute to the organization.

The performance review is also a matchless opportunity to help employees understand their role in executing the agency's branding initiatives. Here are a few examples:

- Participate in the creation of a new employee orientation program.
- Help with the development of a new agency training program.
- Take part in defining new selection criteria for new employees.
- Lead the development of a new employee handbook.

It will take all hands on deck to bring the agency's brand to life. The performance review is your opportunity to get help and support – one employee at a time.

7 **Internal communication.** *Are we using all available means to communicate our positioning with the agency staff?*

It can be argued that the most important quality of leadership is communication. In fact, a fair number of studies show that the leading predictor of success in business is not intelligence, experience, or even enthusiasm – it's *communication skills.*[3]

THE EFFECTIVE STAFF MEETING

Don't make staff meetings a special occasion. If your agency is small enough, gather the troops on a regular basis and keep up the communication.

Product
Brief review of current work
Client results report
New or improved services or capabilities

People
Outstanding efforts and accomplishments
New people
New roles and responsibilities
Open positions
Upcoming agency meetings, training sessions, and events

Process
Changes or improvements to billing or job processing system
Workload, scheduling, and production priorities

Promotion
Recent new business wins
Current new business prospects
Recent agency publicity
Newsworthy stories or work

Place
Office administration updates and reminders

Remember that staff meetings are a superb opportunity to recognize performance, share information, motivate the troops, and have some fun.

Communicating with your staff isn't difficult, but it does take time and discipline. One way to keep your staff informed and involved is to issue a regular company-wide e-mail that reports on the initiatives the agency is undertaking to refocus its brand. While you're at it, you can give a brief update of what's happening in the agency – current client successes, outstanding employee performance, new business activity, etc.

Sometimes the most overlooked form of communication with the staff is the simple staff meeting. Staff meetings shouldn't just be for special occasions. If the agency is too large to gather the entire office, encourage meetings by department or division. Report on the progress you're making in each of the agency's five practice areas – product, people, process, promotion, and place.

HOW THE BEST AGENCIES DO IT

Your people are the key ingredient in bringing your agency brand to life. Unless you have their buy-in and participation, the agency's purpose, principles, and positioning will be worth only the paper they're written on. Aligning your people with your positioning is crucial. Beyond that, here are some other important "people" practices that make agencies successful.

THEY DON'T JUST TALK ABOUT COLLABORATION, THEY ACTUALLY PRACTICE IT

There's nothing agency managers want more than to get their people to work peace-fully and effectively together. But very often agency "teams" are no more than groups of individuals who come together for a status meeting every week. Otherwise, members of the "team" are in their own cubicles, producing their own work.

In the book *Organizing Genius*, business observer Warren Bennis tells stories of "Great Groups" – teams of people at ordinary companies who have accomplished extraordinary things. It's fashionable (especially in agencies) to talk about teams, teamwork, and team spirit. "Yet," says Bennis, "despite the rhetoric of collaboration, we continue to advocate it in a culture in which people strive to distinguish themselves as individuals. We continue to live in a by-line culture where recognition and status are accorded to individuals, not groups."[4]

Getting teams to work together isn't just a matter of encouragement – it's a matter of restructuring the agency in a way that actually makes teams responsible and account-able not just for the work, but for results. (The "dedicated team" concept in use at some agencies is one way to accomplish this.)

As long as your people think that agency management is responsible, they will work more from a paradigm of carrying out orders than taking command. Getting teams to work on their own requires real delegation on your part. Delegating tasks is easy. But delegating *responsibility* is difficult. Delegating the *rights* that go along with that responsibility is downright painful. Agencies that grow and flourish are agencies where the principals have learned to let go.

What applies to individuals also applies to teams. To create "Great Groups" within your agency, delegate the responsibility – and the accompanying rights – for your clients' success.

THEY ADD TALENT, NOT PEOPLE

Every agency has its stars, its key players who usually lead the charge. Once agencies have a few of these people, they then set out to add some "bench strength" – people who can support the star players. This approach to staffing can work sometimes. On championship basketball teams, the bench players are often indistinguishable from the starters. The whole darn team is good, which is one of the big reasons they win their games. But too many agencies are content with only mediocre bench players.

It starts with the belief in strength in *numbers*. If we were running an army, strength in numbers would be very important. But we're running an ad agency, and in a creative enterprise there is only strength in *talent*.

Which would you rather have, one *brilliant* account executive or two average ones? One art director that produces spectacular work, or two art directors that produce average work? One exceptional media planner, or two that would be considered just O.K.? Agencies, like other companies, often make the mistake hiring quantity over quality. As Peter Drucker says, "You should never hire people whose main qualifications are their lack of major weaknesses." The goal, according to Drucker, isn't well-rounded people, but people with real strengths where you need them.[5]

Every business looks for "good people." But in a creative enterprise, what do "good people" look like? In addition to having the knowledge and skills to perform their craft:

> ## In a creative enterprise, there is no strength in numbers. There is only strength in talent.

1. They are passionate about the business. (You can tell the difference between a person who has an average interest in the business and someone who is truly zealous about it. Why not hire the passionate one?)
2. They are able to temper talent and unconventional thinking with maturity and sound judgment.
3. They have the patience to work within a client's current paradigm, while working to help them see a new and better way.
4. They respect the views of co-workers and clients, even if they strongly disagree.

Agency legend David Ogilvy ran recruitment ads looking for "Trumpeter Swans who combine personal genius with inspiring leadership." When you're in a mad scramble for more help, it's difficult to resist the temptation to make do with ugly ducklings. But in the long run, the agencies with the best track records add talent, not people.

THEY ARE FOCUSED ON THE STRENGTHS OF THEIR PEOPLE, NOT THEIR WEAKNESSES

When agency principals meet behind closed doors, wait long enough and their topic of conversation inevitably turns to underperforming employees. The question is are their employees really underperforming, or are they just in the wrong job? Research by The Gallup Organization shows that the vast majority of employees feel miscast in their jobs. Gallup's Marcus Buckingham advises executives, "Think of people management as casting. In business, as in movies, casting is everything. If a good person consistently underachieves in his role, even after encouragement and training, the likely reason is that his talents don't match his role. He is miscast."[6]

In other words, we need to set people up for success – not failure – by putting them in positions where their strengths are maximized and their weaknesses are minimized. This applies even to veterans on your staff who may be in management jobs they simply aren't cut out for. (More on this later.)

Even David Ogilvy acknowledged his inability to be good at everything. In a memo to his senior managers in 1971, he wrote:

> "Long ago I realized that I lack competence, or interest, or both, in several areas of our business. Notably television programming, finance, administration, commer-

cial production and marketing. So I hired people who are strong in those areas where I am weak.

> "Every one of you … is strong in some areas, weak in others. Take my advice: get people alongside you who make up for your weaknesses. If you are strong in production and weak in strategy, have a strategist as your right arm. If you are strong on strategy and weak in production, have a production genius as your right arm. Don't compound your own weaknesses by employing people in key positions who have the *same* weakness."[7]

Focusing on strengths also means accepting that, just like companies, nobody is good at *everything.* As previously discussed, that's the primary fallacy of conventional performance reviews in which the employee is expected to be both creative *and* organized, a good strategist *and* a strong people-person, and other sometimes mutually contradictory qualities.

If you have people with exceptional talents, chances are they will also have exceptional weaknesses. (In fact, these weaknesses are likely to be mirror images of their strengths.) The sooner you accept that fact, the happier you'll be as a manager. The top-performing agencies don't waste their emotional energy complaining about how their people don't do their jobs. Instead, they place them in positions where they can succeed and focus their efforts on building their personal strengths, not "correcting" their personal weaknesses.

Why do we tend to characterize employees by their weaknesses instead of their strengths? Because that's how our managers treated us as we were coming up through the ranks. But you can stop the cycle and transform your company's approach to employee development into something better.

Build on strengths, instead of fretting about weaknesses.

"Too many companies believe people are interchangeable," observes Warren Bennis. "Truly gifted people never are. They have unique talents. Such people cannot be forced into roles they are not suited for, nor should they be. Effective leaders allow great people to do the work they were born to do."[8] Or, as Jim Mullen observes, "It is far less frustrating and more productive to refine a job description to suit its occupant's nature than to get a willful adult to change her lifelong habits."[9]

When you think about it, most agencies have two kinds of account executives:

1. The account executive with a track record for getting jobs produced on time and on budget, but no real talent for thinking strategically.
2. The account executive who writes brilliant strategies and creative briefs, but falls down on logistics, administration, and keeping the client happy.

Agencies usually also have two kinds of copywriters:

1. The writer who develops outstanding concepts, but stumbles when it comes to body copy or long-form writing.
2. The writer who turns out excellent text, but doesn't contribute much to the development of concepts.

Every person brings a different set of awareness, ability, and aptitude to the job. The awareness and ability parts can be improved through training and coaching. But when it comes to *aptitude* – a person's innate abilities – that's where management must make sure each person has a job description that makes the most of strengths and neutralizes weaknesses. If a talented art director just can't keep track of timesheets, get him the help of an assistant who can. If a gifted account planner does a great job of gathering consumer insights but a poor job of turning them into a client presentation, pair her up with a writer who can.
Don't throw the baby out with the bathwater.

THEY CONCENTRATE ON THEIR BEST PEOPLE, NOT THEIR WORST

Do you find it a bit paradoxical that you give more attention to your underperforming employees than you do to your top performers? The rationale is convincing: good people can work on their own, but weak people need help. But ask yourself, which kinds of employees have the most potential to contribute to the success of the organization? Answer: the ones with the most talent.

It's counterintuitive, but the more time you spend with your best people (instead of your worst) the more you can work to leverage their exceptional talents to the benefit of the agency. And there's an even more important reason. Great managers *study* their best people. If you can identify the characteristics of your top performers in your organization, then you'll know what kinds of people to hire in the future.

THEY ACHIEVE ACCOUNTABILITY BY CLARIFYING EXPECTATIONS

Topping the list of "people" concerns in a lot of shops is the issue of accountability. "Nobody around here is accountable," protests the agency CEO as he picks up yet another dropped ball. Meanwhile the culture seems to say, "Firings will continue until morale improves." Well-ordered agencies know that clarifying expectations is the cornerstone of accountability. It's true in personal relationships, client relationships, and employee/manager relationships. Sadly, many agency managers are either too afraid or too busy to outline clear expectations for their staff members. The result is always the same: disappointment that employees aren't doing their job.

If you want to improve accountability at your agency (instead of just worry about it), take the time to discuss your expectations with your employees. Incorporate them into the employee's performance review, which then becomes a kind of agreement between manager and em-

You should keep secrets from your competitors, not your employees.

ployee. Stephen Covey believes the development of such an agreement is the central activity of management. "With an agreement in place, employees can manage themselves within the framework of that agreement," he says. "The manager then can serve like a pace car in a race. He can get things going and then get out of the way. His job from then on is to remove the oil spills."[10]

Performance objectives are the heart of the performance review. At least every six months, ask your employees to review in writing how they did on their performance objectives. Meet to discuss their self-evaluation, give your own input, then agree on performance objectives for the next six-month period. This process of clarifying expectations and evaluating results is actually a very positive and productive experience – for both parties. It breaks the cycle of employees not understanding what management expects of them, and management being constantly disappointed that employees are not living up to expectations.

If it sounds simple, that's because it is. Commit to doing this with all employees for one year, and you'll never go back.

THEY FOCUS ON WHAT THEY CAN DO, NOT WHAT THEY CAN'T DO

It may sound trite to say that successful people are opportunity-minded, not problem-minded, but it's true. It's also true for successful agencies. The countless hours agency principals spend obsessing about problems with their people and clients could be spent much more productively talking about opportunities with their people and clients.

Do you enjoy being around people who are fixated on their problems? Neither do your employees. I once worked with an agency principal who was known to say "I really hate this business" on a fairly regular basis. Of course, such a comment usually inspires nervous laughter among the staff, but eventually they get the message; their boss really does hate this business.

It's the job of an agency leader to *inspire* their troops. To be optimistic rather than fatalistic. Napoleon saw himself as a "dealer in hope." Give your staff hope – a motivating vision of what the agency can become. Who would have thought a tiny start-up in a town like Minneapolis would grow to become one of the most well-known, respected shops in the business? Fallon is now practically a household word in the business world. And their reputation is as stellar as ever. They didn't get that way by obsessing about their problems. Neither did Weiden & Kennedy, TBWA/Chiat/Day, or The Martin Agency.

As Henry Ford said, "If you think you can't, you're right. And if you think you can, you're right."

THEY KNOW THE DIFFERENCE BETWEEN MANAGEMENT TALENT AND FUNCTIONAL TALENT

It doesn't matter how many times we see the oft-touted "Peter Principle" at play, we continue to promote people with absolutely no aptitude for management into management positions. Why? Because they have "earned" it. They put in their time as an art director, so now it's time to make them a creative director. They were brilliant as an art director. But now they're a near disaster as a creative director. Sound familiar?

Solution number one: live through two or three years of frustration, after which you either terminate the employee or he leaves anyway. Solution number two: try to give the employee some management skills by sending him to a few seminars for creative directors, hoping this will produce a change in behavior. Solution number three: realize that you've made a mistake, and offer to give the employee his old job back with no reduction in salary.

None of these solutions seem very appealing, do they? Yet this is what happens day in and day out at most agencies. You can break this cycle with one simple but unconventional change in your thinking: *Create a career path for exceptional people who wouldn't make good managers.*

The problem in the traditional staffing scenario is that as people advance through their careers, once they reach a certain level in their functions they have nowhere to go but into a management position. What about giving these employees other symbols of success instead, such as more money (perhaps as much as a manager) or a better title? You can find ways to bestow physical and psychological rewards on your best people without necessarily elevating them into a management position. The agencies that think this way don't really *want* to put their best professionals in management, because then they will lose the tremendous contributions these people make to their respective crafts — account planning, media, creative, etc.

You can give more money and more prestige to your best performers without making them managers. It's a revolutionary thought, but the people who are excellent in their disciplines should have the ability to earn as much as their managers. In some very progressive

Create a career path for exceptional people who wouldn't make good managers.

companies, star performers can even earn *more* than the people who manage them. To confer public prestige (which most good people crave and deserve), use a system of titles that connotes the levels of expertise individuals have reached in their disciplines.

"Agencies take their top creative talent and promote them into management roles where they don't get to do the work anymore," says GSD&M leader Roy Spence.[11] To allow creative directors to do what they do best – create – GSD&M created the position of "creative operations director," which handles the administrative duties usually reserved for the executive creative director; including work distribution, dispute mediation, hiring, and firing.

In the agency business, we constantly encourage our clients to break the rules. So go ahead and break one of your own. Don't make ascension to management an automatic career path. Keep your best people happy doing what they do best.

THEY TREAT THEIR EMPLOYEES (PARTICULARLY THEIR CREATIVES) LIKE THEIR BEST CLIENTS

Think of it this way: your employees don't work for you, you work for them. They're the reason you're successful. They keep the jobs going, the income flowing, and the business growing. Sought-after agencies treat their employees with courtesy, encouragement, and respect.

This is crucial in a business that employs artists – writers, art directors, creative directors, etc. While artists like money just like everyone else, it's not the reason they come into work every day. They come for psychological rewards. The currency of their trade is acknowledgment, appreciation, and admiration. Talented creatives are repelled by authoritarian management styles, which is why agencies with a "master and servant" management approach never make it onto the national scene.

When you start each business day, ask yourself what you can do to help your employees, not what they can do to help you.

THEY HAVE AN OPEN-BOOK APPROACH TO AGENCY MANAGEMENT

Nowhere is it lonelier at the top than in an advertising agency. Agency presidents voice chronic complaints about lack of interest and participation from staff members in managing the affairs of the agency. The problem, in most cases, isn't lack of interest. It's lack of involvement.

Winning agencies involve their employees in management issues by informing and delegating. It's far better to err on the side of sharing too much information than not enough. Playing agency finances close to the vest is an outmoded management style, born in the bygone era of command-and-control management. If you want your employees to care, share. Share in staff meetings, in team meetings, in management team meetings. Share income and expenses, windfalls and write-offs, profit and loss. Share everything except salaries. You'll be amazed at the level of commitment that comes from a staff that feels involved. One of the real innovators in the school of "open-book management" is business CEO Jack Stack who explored the topic in his book *The Great Game of Business*. Says Stack:

> "The more people know about a company, the better that company will perform. This is an iron-clad rule. You will always be more successful in business by sharing information with the people you work with than by keeping them in the dark. Let your people know whatever you know about the company, the division, the department, the particular task at hand. Information should not be a power tool – it should be a means of education. Don't use information to intimidate, control, or manipulate people. Use it to teach people how to work together to achieve common goals and thereby gain control over their lives. When you share the numbers and bring them alive, you turn them into tools people can use to help themselves as they go about their business every day. That's the key to open-book management."[12]

Using these principles, Stack turned his own company into one of the most profitable in America – and this is a manufacturing company, staffed largely by hourly workers. Imagine how open-book management can work with a professional services firm. When you share your income, expenses, and profit or loss, you make your employees part of the solution instead of part of the problem.

In surveys fielded among agency employees, scores on the question "I feel vested in the financial success of the agency" are consistently low. How can employees feel like they make a financial difference if they really don't know how the agency is doing?

The first step in open-book management is to teach your staff how the agency makes money. This may seem elementary, but it's surprising how enlightening this is for most employees. Then, share your key monthly and year-to-date financial results with as many employees as possible – in staff meetings, department meetings, management team meetings, or whatever venue works best for your agency. You can do this by developing a *financial scorecard* that tracks key measures of success (see end of chapter).

HOW ONE AGENCY ALIGNED THEIR PEOPLE WITH THEIR POSITIONING

A small but progressive agency in the Northeastern U.S. had all the right ingredients – and the right location – to support a positioning that focused on outdoor recreation. They described their positioning in a single word: Play. Their goal was to become one of the recognized experts in the eyes of companies that market to people who love to play (ski, hike, bike, climb, etc.). Here are a few quotes from their internal branding document, "People at Play."

Every impression our people make on prospects, clients, and the community should reinforce our new Play positioning.

Playful Dress Code. Employees are encouraged to dress casually, including jeans and t-shirts. (Casual dress is less restrictive, more creative, and projects a Play mentality. Also, many of our Play clients dress similarly.)

Playful Employee Bios. When composing bios for new business purposes, describe our Play lives as well as our professional lives. (This will contribute to our credibility as Play experts.)

Hire People Who Play. Recruit Playful people using alternative media, such as sports or recreation media. When all else is equal, hire the employee that is an avid Player. (This contributes to our Play expertise.)

Play On The First Day. Make a new employee's first day a Play experience through activities such as hiking, biking, climbing, etc. with their supervisor. Give them a "welcome box" filled with Play items such as a sports nutrition bar, sports drink, keys to the company Jeep, etc. (What better way to show that we walk our talk.)

Build Playful Client Teams. When we get a new client, invite our key client contacts to participate with us in a ropes course or other team-building exercise. (Building a client

(Continued on next page)

Open-book management has the potential to help you far more than it can hurt you. You should keep secrets from your competitors, not your employees.

THEY RUN LEAN

I once overheard an agency manager say that the best way to hire 100 good people is to hire 200. If you think that's funny, consider that some agencies actually operate this way. They end up with far more people than they really need, putting a constant drain on agency profitability.

There's no argument that running in a slightly lean mode makes for a profitable agency. But does it also make for a happier one? It's somewhat illogical but true that agency people are usually happier and more fulfilled when the agency is slightly understaffed instead of overstaffed.

Actually, it's not so illogical if you think about it. If you're running lean, it challenges people more because it gives them more responsibility. More importantly, it gives them less idle time (and you know what they say about idle time). People who are busy fill their days with productive work. People who *aren't* busy end up gossiping about other people or just getting in their way. It's one of those unfortunate aspects of human nature. As George Washington said, "My observation is that whenever one person is found adequate to the discharge of a duty by close application thereto, it is worse executed by two persons, and scarcely done at all if three or more are employed therein."

When it comes to people, fewer is often better.

THEY DON'T USE TECHNOLOGY AS A SUBSTITUTE FOR TALENT

No one in the agency business would disagree that technology has completely changed the way we do our jobs. Long gone are the days of using a knife and glue to produce an ad. Thanks to highly specialized hardware and software, we work faster and our reproduction quality is better.

But with the advent of new technology has come a new set of issues. The real advantage of technology is that it allows a talented art director to explore more options and ultimately end up with a better product. The disadvantage is that people with only modest talent, by virtue of owning a Macintosh, believe they are

relations model where the agency and client are literally on one team reinforces our Play positioning and sets the stage for rewarding relationships.)

Leave A Day To Play. Allow the option of occasionally working ten-hour, four-day weeks, to leave a day to play. (This is a statement about our commitment to the importance of Play.)

Playful Messages On Hold. Callers on hold should hear Play messages (songs, excerpts from books, etc. (Another opportunity to reinforce our brand.)

Play Profiles. Display profiles of our people in the lobby, placing special emphasis on their Play experience, including photos, postcards, etc. (This demonstrates that we do what we say – we Play.)

Play-Full Lockers. Install lockers in a prominent places that are filled with Play equipment like Frisbees, balls, etc. for use by employees and clients. (This establishes a playful atmosphere and encourages people to Play.)

Train to Play. As part of our professional development program, occasionally include a topic such as "How to telemark." (We need to continually sharpen our professional and Play skills.)

Give to Organizations That Play. Perform pro bono work only for organizations that encourage or support Play. (This demonstrates our own support for Play.)

Showcase Play. Hold a yearly eco-challenge event, sponsored by the agency. (Reinforces our positioning and gets us great press.)

creatively brilliant. For all its extraordinary benefits, a Macintosh does not an art director make. We now unfortunately have a whole new crop of instant desktop art directors, who are proving the Peter Principle has broken into the computer age.

Equipped with an electronic-generated palette, non-art directors are art directing. A photograph is manipulated not because it should be, but because it can be. Stars, pin dots, and palettes of shading are not used because of their intrinsic value, but because they exist in a software package.

Writer Aldous Huxley once said it is "…far easier to write ten passably effective Sonnets…than one effective advertisement." Anybody can get on a computer, put in some words, add some images and call it an ad. But the ability to produce strong, memorable concepts is still something technology cannot accomplish. Which makes recruiting for *talent* – not just computer skills – an increasingly important consideration in staffing.

And then there's e-mail, perhaps the biggest time waster in business. Most employees spend more time checking, responding to, and deleting e-mail messages than accomplishing the important tasks of the day. Walk into any office at random, any time of day, and there is at least a 50/50 chance the occupants will be looking through their e-mail.

The real dark side of e-mail is the effect it has had on personal interaction in the agency. Some agencies have finally put their foot down on the use of e-mail for routine communication. "E-mail less, walk more," says Richards Group founder Stan Richards. "Get up. Walk to the desk of the person you want to speak to. At the very least, pick up the phone and call the person on the intercom if you're really in a big hurry. But no internal e-mails."[13]

E-mail should be completely banned as a tool for waging electronic warfare. Using e-mail to scold or criticize another employee is inhumane. These are the situations in which face-to-face communication is *most* important. Hiding behind e-mail erodes the trust and mutual respect you're trying to cultivate in your organization.

THEY LEAD THE CHARGE

"In the year of our Lord 1314, patriots of Scotland, starving and outnumbered, charged the fields of Bannockburn. They fought like warrior poets. They fought like Scotsmen. And won their freedom." So begins the film *Braveheart*. William Wallace painted his face blue and led the charge – literally. He was at the head of his rag-tag band of freedom fighters.

While the battle agencies fight is a little less life-threatening, it still requires leaders who are willing to lead the charge. It requires being on the front lines with the rest of the team, in hand-to-hand combat for the success of the agency and its clients. It means setting the example.

Too many agency principals engage in armchair leadership, telling their soldiers instead of showing them. Worse, they behave as though they are above the law. They themselves come to the office late, then berate their underlings for tardiness. They leave early to see their son's soccer games but criticize their employees for their low billable time. They lead the kind of privileged lifestyle that makes armies turn on their officers, like a scene from *Mutiny on the Bounty.*

Meanwhile, the agencies that are famous for their work are also famous for the work ethic of their leaders. They are the Jeff Goodby's and Rich Silverstein's of the world — people who are totally dedicated to their craft and inspire their staff by working harder than everyone else instead of taking the afternoon off to play golf.

There's a valuable lesson in the old Chinese proverb, "Tell me and I'll forget; show me and I may remember; involve me and I'll understand."

What changes do you need to make to your promotion, new business, and publicity program to bring your positioning to life?

7 PROMOTION:
Making New Business A Game You're Favored To Win

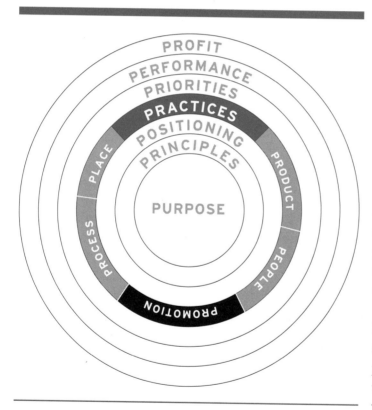

FOR ADVERTISING agencies, promotion is the most obvious way to build a brand — except that they're usually thinking in terms of their clients' brands, not their own. The old adage that the cobbler's children have the poorest shoes certainly applies to agencies. They usually produce good work for their clients and poor work for themselves.

Here's how to turn your agency's considerable promotional skills inward to make promotion of your own firm a strength instead of a weakness.

1 **New business approach.** *Given our positioning, what should be our new business approach?*

Start by asking, "What if we were our own client?" How would you describe your communications objective? Your target audience? Your key benefit? In other words, how would you write a creative brief for your own agency brand? Gather your best strategic minds together and draft answers to the following.

> *Business Objective.* What business or marketing objective are you trying to accomplish with your agency self-promotion and new business program?
>
> *Market Situation.* What is the current market situation and how does your agency brand fit in?
>
> *Brand Strengths.* What are the important rational or emotional characteristics of your agency brand, and what makes it different or better than other agency brands?
>
> *Target Prospect.* Who are your most promising prospective clients, and what do you know about their awareness, attitudes, or experience?
>
> *Communications Objective.* What do you want prospective clients to think, feel or do as a result of your communication with them?
>
> *Competitive Frame.* Who or what else do you compete with – either directly or indirectly?
>
> *Key Message.* What is the single idea you want to communicate to prospective clients?

Remember that your goal isn't to show how you're just like other leading agencies. It's to show how you are different. You can't try too hard in this area. As positioning proponent Jack Trout says, "You can't overcommunicate your difference."[1]

2 Prospective clients. *What specific criteria should we apply to prospective clients?*

Unless an agency is focused, it almost always makes the mistake of considering everyone to be a prospective client. Consider the many times you have asked a new client, "Who is your target audience?" and their answer is "Everybody." You then diplomatically explain to your client that "everybody" is not really a target audience, particularly since your client makes mechanical components for jet fighters.

Funny as it seems, most agencies still consider "everybody" as a prospect. Any company with money – from here to Istanbul – qualifies. Sometimes, any client that's breathing qualifies. You would never advise your clients to pursue such a strategy. Why do it yourself?

After months of self-reflection, a West Coast agency realized that not only are they business-to-business specialists (they hadn't really realized it before), they actually built most of their client experience with a particular kind of B-to-B client. Talk to their new business guy and he'll tell you how their database of prospective clients went from 4,000 names to 400, and how they arrived at very specific criteria for determining who's a prospect and who's not.

They seek clients who spend from $1 million to $10 million, located in the Western U.S., who market products and services that would be considered complex, considered purchases (like mechanical components for jet fighters). On top of that, they have a specific strategy for helping what would be considered "challenger brands" (brands that are not yet leaders in their category), so they also add this to their list of criteria for prospective clients.

Does this limit their success? On the contrary, it enhances it. Every time this agency pitches this kind of client, they're playing to the agency's strengths. Their chances of winning are much higher than the scores of "generalist" agencies that attempt to throw their hats into any ring that comes along.

Your goal isn't to show how you're just like the other leading agencies. It's to show how you are different.

Another agency on the other side of the U.S. discovered that most of their core competencies are in the retail arena, which led them to develop a rather unique set of criteria for prospective clients. They actively seek 1) Businesses that depend on driving consumers to a location to make a purchase 2) Whose marketing objective is to make lifetime customers through repeat purchases, and 3) Who use a media-intensive marketing approach. Does this sound too limiting? Consider that this definition could apply not only to a national retail chain, but to a hospital system, or even a local bank. Put this agency in a review for this type of client and the odds are overwhelmingly in their favor. They have strong credentials, strong experience, and a strong knowledge base in this area.

You only get so many times at bat. Why not play in a game where you're favored to win?

3 Corporate identity. *How does our agency brand impact on our corporate identity standards?*

While the answer to this question seems self-evident, it's remarkable how many agencies fail to manifest their brand identity in their own printed and online materials. In fact, agencies are among the worst – not the best – examples of consistent corporate identity.

The computer age has only hurt, not helped. At least in the days of pre-printed forms, the agency logo and typeface were prominently displayed on memos, conference reports, status reports, and insertion orders. But look at most agency correspondence today and you'll see a mish-mash of assorted formats and typefaces, with the agency logo noticeably absent much of the time. Conference reports issued by one account executive look nothing like those issued by another. Memos to clients look like they have been designed by Microsoft instead of the agency – because they have. This is not the example agencies should set for the companies to whom they preach branding.

What's the most common form of correspondence in today's agency? E-mail. What is the most generic-looking, least branded form of communication in today's agency? E-mail. If you want to set a good example for your clients, ask your IT department to set up electronic letterhead to be used on all e-mail correspondence. Do the same with all computer-generated forms, faxes, memos, reports, plans, leave-behinds, and recommendations.

4 Self-promotion materials. *What kind of self-promotion materials should we have?*

You would expect that people in the business of communication design would have some of the best credentials materials, when in fact very often they have some of the worst. An agency's approach to self-promotion is often a style or cultural issue. Some firms feel that if you have a sterling reputation, you don't need elaborate promotional materials. But even the most notable agencies are required to submit credentials materials to agency search firms and to prospective clients in the first stages of most agency reviews.

Your promotional materials are the most visible manifestation of your agency brand, so not only should they have the right style, but the right substance. Pay attention first to *what* you say, then how you say it. Don't fall into the trap of having a brochure that looks cool, but fails to make a point. Having a clear positioning, a strong concept, and a unique point of view is ultimately more important than the paper stock or the number of inks.

Warning: the reason most agencies struggle with self-promotion materials is that they are overly ambitious. They have grand plans to do a state-of-the-art Web site, a series of 3-D mailings, an oversized brochure, and a Mariachi band. Problem is, the daily pressures of client business keep them from ever completing these internal projects, and everybody – including the principals – becomes disillusioned about the agency's self-promotion program.

The cure is as obvious as the disease: keep it simple. Most prospective clients have neither the time nor the inclination to wade through a large stack of agency literature. Prospects must be able to quickly scan your credentials materials and get the gist of what you're about without reading every word of copy.

THE BUSINESS DEVELOPMENT PLAN

Most agencies are frustrated by the fact that their clients don't or won't plan. To avoid being guilty of the same sin, here's a checklist of things you should consider in an annual business development plan.

Prior Year in Review
New accounts or assignments won
Presentations to prospects
Meetings with prospects (formal and informal)
Proposals and RFP responses completed
Prospects turned down or referred
Awards won
Press received (print, television, radio, Web)

New Business Program
Current new business objectives and priorities
Criteria for new clients (size, category, location, etc.)
New business database, prospect segmentation and prioritization
Questionnaire and RFP responses development
New business presentation development

Self Promotion Program
Agency brochure, portfolio, reel, and other promotional materials
Web site and internet marketing
Agency advertising
Directory listings (printed and on-line)
Speaking opportunities
Award competitions
Marketing to agency search consultants
Mailings and e-mailings
Community involvement and civic service

Publicity Program
Pitching agency news
Guest columns
Contact and relationship building with reporters and editors
Article reprints

So what kind of promotional materials should you have? You can be wildly creative in this area (and some agencies are), but there are some basic things every agency must have in its self-promotion quiver:

A *one-page introduction letter* that succinctly and persuasively describes the agency. You'll need this letter to accompany credentials materials, proposals, and a host of other things. This may be your most important new business tool, so spend some time with it. Writing a good one-page letter isn't as simple as it sounds.

A *credentials piece* that describes the capabilities, competencies, and experience of the agency. While this piece can take many forms, the important point is to keep it modular, so it can be easily updated and customized. It's more important to be able to show current work, current client lists, and current results than it is to have a pre-printed piece. The quality of digital reproduction these days should allow virtually every piece you produce to be current and customized to the prospective client. What should be in the credentials brochure? This is a tricky question, because the temptation is to include too much information, and most agency brochures end up looking and sounding remarkably alike (not to mention boring). The typical list includes agency history, size, years in business, offices, clients, philosophy, services, biographies, and case studies – you know the drill. Aside from not being very interesting, this approach tends to focus on features instead of *benefits* – the cardinal sin in marketing. Most of all, the credentials brochure must brand your agency and set it apart from the hundreds of other firms all clamoring for the same account. This is not just a matter of making your agency look different; it must also *sound* different. The brochure gives you an opportunity to weave your positioning though literally every aspect of the agency, from the way you describe your services to the way you write your bios and case studies. Help your prospective clients come away with the impression that you are not the same as everyone else; not just because you have a different-looking brochure (style), but because you have a different approach than other agencies (substance).

Examples of your very best work in all major media. For work developed in print media, a large-format booklet still works best. Again, in-house digital printing allows you to customize each piece to each prospect. Show your best TV on a videotape or DVD. Interactive examples should be posted to your Web site.

An agency video that tells the story of the agency and showcases its best work. This is not the same as a TV reel. Many agency search consultants ask for a video to use as a means of introducing the agency to prospective clients. You'll find that the video also serves as a useful tool in sit-down meetings with prospective clients. Just remember the audience; you'll need to show not only creativity, but results. And for no more than seven minutes (which is apparently the attention span of today's business people).

5 Web site. *How does our positioning impact the design and architecture of our Web site?*

Lest we forget, your Web site is actually your most important piece of agency self-promotion. The Web is now the primary source of information for people who want to know more about your agency (including prospective clients and employees). So if you don't make a good showing on the Web, you will have missed your opportunity make a good first impression.

The natural reluctance agencies have to brand themselves is only intensified in the realm of new business.

Needless to say, your Web site must exude the positioning of the agency. And it must be an example of your best thinking and your best creative work, not something that was patched together in haste and then forgotten. Far too many agencies still have an underwhelming presence on the Web.

This doesn't mean you have to develop the Web site yourself. If interactive marketing isn't one of your core competencies, there's no shame in finding a good Web developer to create, host, and maintain your site. Just don't make apologies about it, promising that a new and improved Web site is under construction. (What are your clients supposed to think?) And remember that your Web site is a living, breathing thing – which means someone in your organization needs to have the responsibility to keep it updated with fresh information and creative work.

Finally, remind yourself that the goal of your Web site isn't to show how you're the same as other agencies, but how you're *different.*

6 Agency publicity. *What should we be doing in the area of agency publicity?*

Branding or re-branding your agency presents remarkable opportunities for publicity. Aside from landing some big clients, it's potentially the biggest news you've had since starting the agency. The advertising trade press will naturally be interested. And if your agency brand puts a particularly controversial stake in the ground, the business press will find it newsworthy as well.

RiechesBaird in Irvine, California, found that they were able to achieve status as one of the nation's leading B2B agency brands by implementing an aggressive publicity program. In one year, they went from not showing up on the national radar screen to making the cover of B2B magazine, achieving a ranking in the list of national business-to-business agencies, and being named the leading B2B agency in their region by the business press. Agency principals reinforced this perception of expertise by writing and submitting guest columns, which were published and reprinted.

Isn't it paradoxical that many of the agencies that excel at getting publicity for their clients fail to put their energies into getting publicity for themselves? Conversely, some agencies with no formal public relations department excel at achieving notoriety for their work. Don't be lulled into thinking that somehow it's a matter of luck. The agencies you see regularly in the trade and business press work devilishly hard at it. If you apply the same kind of effort, you'll get the same kind of results.

7 Unconventional marketing approaches. *What unconventional self-promotion methods could we consider to support our agency brand?*

When it comes to agency news, sometimes the best approach is to make your own. Does your rebranding effort give you the opportunity to stage an event or launch a self-promotion campaign that will turn the heads of editors?

DiZinno Thompson in San Diego developed an extraordinary public service campaign and executed it in outdoor bulletins placed in high-traffic freeway locations throughout their headquarters city. While it's not unusual for agencies to do public service outdoor advertising, it is unusual for the campaign to be completely sponsored and paid for by the agency. This meant that the agency could tackle any kind of controversial topic they wanted, so they illustrated the city's problems with guns, condom use, and abuse. The visually arresting boards got the attention not just of the business press, but of the TV stations, the radio talk show hosts, and virtually the entire city.

Agencies can use the same guerilla marketing tactics they recommend to their clients, from painting sides of buildings to paying mimes to stand on street corners. An agency with an emphasis on outdoor recreation decided to establish a triathlon in their home town. Some shops have created their own branded line of clothing. An agency in Salt Lake City formerly known as Dahlin Smith White (DSW) produced shirts and jackets with the DSW label, only in this case the initials stood for something more interesting: Do Something Wild. They sold through mail order and even had a booth at NBA games.

A few London agencies have gone so far as to open their own retail stores stocked with agency-branded products. Who would think that the brand names of professional services firms would enter pop culture?

> **Agencies that are too busy to develop a new business program inevitably need new business.**

Great agencies make their clients' brands famous. Why not try to do the same thing for your own?

HOW THE BEST AGENCIES DO IT

A common characteristic of well-known agencies is that they actively market their agency brand. They're famous not just because they do great work (although that certainly helps), but because they follow a set of best practices in the area of agency self-promotion.

THEY MAKE AGENCY PROMOTION SOMETHING THAT HAPPENS ON PURPOSE

Imagine an accounting firm that does a lousy job of keeping its own books, or an architectural firm housed in a dilapidated building, and you have the equivalent of an advertising agency with no self-promotion program.

The common defense for this is simply "We don't have time; we're too busy working on our clients' business." While it's good and noble to be occupied with your clients' interests, it can be a little bit like the dentist who is so busy caring for his patient's teeth that he neglects to brush his own.

Agencies that are too busy to develop a new business program inevitably need new business.

A more tenable excuse is "The work should speak for itself." Unquestionably, producing great work is your agency's most valuable new business tool. But it is not a new business *program.* Most great creative shops systematically publicize their work. Most actively market themselves to agency search consultants. Most have a dedicated new business development person. And they all work at building a network of relationships that can turn into clients someday. Divest yourself of the notion that the agencies that are successful in new business are just lucky. Behind their seemingly fortuitous wins is a conscious effort to build their agency brand.

THE AGENCY PROMOTION MANAGER

In addition to a director of business development, a manager of agency promotion can focus on the myriad things most agencies "never get around to," including:

- Oversee agency corporate identity and graphic standards.
- Develop and administer the new business database.
- Oversee self-promotion materials (brochures, reels, portfolios, etc.).
- Supervise agency Web site.
- Update and maintain agency directory listings (printed and on-line).
- Manage agency mailings.
- Coordinate the development of proposals and RFP responses.
- Organize speaker's bureau program.
- Collect and maintain agency work samples.
- Lead the agency publicity program (new clients, new campaigns, new people, new work, etc.)

THEY HAVE A PROACTIVE, NOT REACTIVE, NEW BUSINESS PROGRAM

Should the agency CEO be personally involved in new business? Yes. Should he or she personally head up the new business program? No. While new business may be the lifeblood of the agency, the CEO is responsible for administering other forms of critical care, namely the leadership and management of the agency. In order to make new business something that actually happens instead of something that just gets talked about, agencies need an experienced business development person.

The absolute worst way to organize a new business program is for the CEO to pronounce that "New business is everyone's responsibility." As every experienced businessperson knows, if everyone is responsible, then no one is responsible. It's actually the best way to insure that nothing gets done.

On the other hand, having a dedicated person with "business development" in his or her title means you have someone who is looking for new clients while you're taking care of the ones you already have.

THEY MAKE THE MOST OF THEIR POINT OF DIFFERENCE

It must be a curious thing for clients to sit through a string of new business presentations by agencies all claiming essentially the same things: unequalled strategic brilliance, unsurpassed creative prowess, and unparalleled media leverage. But as with great advertising, great agencies focus on what makes them different, not what makes them the same.

"The common failing among agencies seeking new business," says agency search consultant Bob Lundin, "is their inability or unwillingness to name what they stand for and market themselves on distinguishable differences." He advises agencies to come to terms with their strengths and weaknesses and establish a brand just as recognizable as that of any client.[2]

What makes your agency different to prospective clients is likely what you *think*, not what you have. It's not that you have a research department with combined experience of 170 years, it's that you use innovative methods for uncovering the emotional elements of consumer wants and needs. It's not that you have a 32-person media department with access to all the major media databases, it's that you follow a distinctive media planning approach that values the quality of a media vehicle's audience more than its size.

Standing out in new business situations means having a distinctive point of view. A few of the more progressive agency search consultants advise agencies to view their "capabilities brochure" as a "point of view brochure" instead. Yes, your self-promotion literature may still have to spell out the agency's size, structure, and experience (the things that make you the same as other agencies), but your *main* messages should be about the unique ways you approach your client's business (the things that make you different).

THEY TALK IN TERMS OF CLIENT BENEFITS, NOT AGENCY FEATURES

The advertising axiom "People don't buy quarter-inch drill bits, they buy quarter-inch holes," relates every bit as well to the way advertising agencies sell themselves. Clients buy the benefit of working with your agency, not the agency's features. They buy an agency that can help them increase brand awareness and sales, not an agency with two offices, 150 employees and a proud 25-year history.

This is, of course, the same advice you give to clients who insist on an advertising campaign that talks about what *they* want instead of what their *customer* wants. All advertising professionals know that successful messaging isn't about what the company wants to say, it's about what the consumer wants to hear. It's not about what the company wants; it's about what the consumer wants.

Professional rainmaker Ford Harding tells the story of presenting as a young consultant to the president of a large corporation. During the presentation, Ford was interrupted three times by the company president asking, "Why is this important to my company?" The lesson he learned stuck with him the rest of his career: you persuade by focusing on benefits.[3]

If you want to revolutionize your new business approach, simply apply this same thinking to your agency. While this may appear to be a blinding glimpse of the obvious, precious few agencies muster the discipline to do it. It's just too tempting

GETTING THE BUSINESS BEFORE THE PITCH

If you subscribe to the school of thought that believes most new business is won before the pitch, here are 20 ways to make sure you have all the bases covered.

1. Gather all existing secondary information.
2. Call media reps and editors for info about client, competitors, and key issues.
3. Collect information from client industry associations.
4. Review key trade publications.
5. Collect media spending data.
6. Read books about the client's business.
7. Find a contact inside the client company.
8. Research background of individuals in presentation.
9. Collect and analyze client ads and competitive ads.
10. Identify the most important client problems, issues, wants and needs.
11. Interview the "field."
12. Meet with senior client management.
13. Talk to the account executive of the outgoing agency.
14. Hire an industry consultant and pick his or her brain.
15. Develop an "issues page" to brief the new business team.
16. Hold focus groups and invite the client to attend.
17. Prepare videotaped interviews with consumers or other important audiences.
18. If possible, pre-present creative ideas to the main client contact.
19. Send an advance presentation agenda in "invitation" form.
20. Ask referral sources to call and recommend you.

to fall back on the self-centered approach of talking about agency history, size, structure, departments, capabilities, experience, zzzzzzzzzz.

Hence the biggest problem with agency promotional literature: too much "us" and not enough "them." You've got to muster the discipline to relate absolutely everything you say to the client and their wants, needs, and desired results – not agency capabilities. Forget about what *you* want and focus on what *they* want. Aside from your positioning and distinctive philosophies, this alone will set you apart from 99% of the other agencies in the world.

In new business and self-promotion, always apply the "so what" test. When you make a point to a prospective client, ask yourself if this is a client benefit or merely an agency feature. Agency features are important to agencies. Client benefits are important to clients.

The brains behind the famous "got milk?" campaign encourages advertising people to think about the times as kids when they wanted to ask their parents for money or ask someone out on a date. How did they approach the problem? What worked? What didn't?

> "Most people agree that a simple statement of one's intentions has the odds stacked against it, and a demand that your parents hand over the cash or that the lady or gentleman in question gives you his or her heart or body before even knowing your name is unlikely to yield either financial or romantic satisfaction. In the end, the majority agrees that the only way to increase your chance of success is to mentally step out of your shoes and into theirs. What is currently stopping them from writing you a check or falling into your arms? What could you do or say to remove those barriers? And most significant of all, what could you do or say to make your parents decide *for themselves* that they want to give you a spot bonus, or cause the object of your wildest dreams to develop an uncontrollable crush on you?"[4]

When it comes to orienting new business presentations around client benefits (instead of agency features), the bravest move you can make is not only to save agency credentials for the very end of the new business presentation, but to consider not presenting agency credentials at all. Clients don't really care about most agency credentials in the first place, and they will care even less if you've done a good job of showing them how you can solve their problems.

THEY SHOW INSTEAD OF TELL

The tried-and-true "demonstration" TV commercial is so effective for the simple reason that it shows the product benefit instead of just claiming it. It's one thing to claim your detergent removes nuclear waste — it's quite another thing to demonstrate it. Just like it's one thing to say your agency gets to the heart of consumer motivations, but it's something else to actually prove it.

> # The boardroom is really no different than the courtroom.
> # Agencies must present convincing evidence to back up their claims.

In new business situations, your time is much better spent demonstrating three things than claiming 30. In court, what jury would be moved to convict a defendant on the basis of glittering generalities from the prosecuting attorney? The boardroom is really no different than the courtroom. Agencies must present convincing evidence to back up their claims of strategic virtuosity, one-of-a-kind inventiveness, and creative infallibility.

So to demonstrate their competence, agencies usually turn to the trusty case study. When should you use case studies? There's a school of thought that says "never," based on the belief that all case studies sound the same and all end in the same predictable successful outcome. (Have you ever seen an agency case study that ends in disaster?) Another school of thought says to use case studies only if they are relevant to the prospective client's business. Yet another school — the one to which I belong — believes that a case study should be used only if it supports one of the main points you're trying to make in your presentation, and only if the problem and the solution can be dramatized in an engaging and memorable way.

Better yet, instead of presenting a "case history" for a past client, present a "case future" for your prospective client, showing how you plan to tackle their thorniest marketing problems and what kind of outcome you predict. Agency search consultant

Mike Marsak regularly recommends this approach to agencies, only to find that a rare few are willing to test it out. There is, he believes, too much safety in the familiar, which is unfortunate for an industry that regularly chides its clients for their unwillingness to forsake convention.

THEY KNOW THAT IN NEW BUSINESS, THE GREATEST RISK IS NO RISK AT ALL

The natural reluctance agencies have to brand themselves — to be willing to stand for something instead of trying to stand for everything — is intensified in the realm of new business. Agencies want to cover all the bases, address all the concerns, and generally present themselves as the cure-all for anything and everything that's ailing the prospective client.

If you were trying to protect your company from a major lawsuit, would you hire a law firm that claims to be good at everything, or one that you know has a great practice in litigation? In politics, would you vote for the candidate who tries to agree with everyone, or the one who takes a firm stand on the important issues of the day? *Time* magazine once observed that the candidates most likely to win the presidency are the ones "confident enough to risk broad, bold themes that capture the national imagination."[5] Agencies that win in new business are the ones willing to plant a few bold stakes in the ground and inspire clients to new heights.

All professional presenters advise a strong opening, and strong closing, and no more than two or three memorable themes for your presentation — themes that are repeated and reinforced through stories and examples. Don't allow yourself to be lulled into believing that if you just do exactly what the client asks on their 15-point list of "What we're looking for in an agency" that you'll win the business. You won't. The agency that inspires the client will.

A dramatic example of this principle in action was the review of the Virgin Atlantic Airways account. As the *New York Times* reported it, "An upstart airline is hiring an upstart agency in an appropriately upstart fashion, awarding the account by abruptly halting a review that was to have run at least another month." The review was to have been narrowed to two finalists, with a winner to be named months later. Instead Virgin Atlantic executives cut short the process, deciding to hire Crispin, Porter & Bogusky on the spot. Why? Because the agency adopted a strong stance that Virgin

THE NEW BUSINESS AUDIT

In new business, knowledge is power. At the beginning of the new business process, do everything you can to gather the following information from your prospective client.

Company

How would you describe the company's mission?

How do your customers perceive you? How do you want your customers to perceive you?

What makes the company/product/service truly different or unique?

What are your primary business objectives?

What are the company/product/service's strengths and weaknesses, both real and perceived?

What are the important opportunities for the company in the future? What are the threats?

How has the company been performing financially?

Marketing

How would you describe the company's marketing approach?

What are your current marketing objectives?

What is currently the company's biggest sales or marketing problem?

What market segments do you sell to (by product, demographics, geography, etc.)?

Products or Services

What are the important characteristics of your products or services?

What are the key benefits of your products or services (rational, sensory and emotional)?

What are the perceived disadvantages of your products or services?

How does your pricing compare with competitors?

What new products or services are planned for the immediate future?

(Continued on next page)

should capitalize on its unconventional brand image by using marketing initiatives that go well beyond the tried-and-true airline TV spots and newspaper ads.[6]

More than ever, what clients are seeking from their agency is not really partnership but *leadership*. They respect the conviction of a strong point of view, and can genuinely use the help in navigating through today's troubled marketing waters.

THEY MARKET THEIR AGENCY BRAND TO ALL THEIR AUDIENCES, NOT JUST POTENTIAL CLIENTS

Smart agencies counsel their clients to think beyond their primary customers and consider the other audiences that can be critical to the success of their brand — employees, the trade, the media, the financial community, etc. Advertising agencies operate in the same environment. Potential clients may be the ultimate destination, but selling the agency to other important audiences is sometimes how you get there.

Agency search consultants are now involved in about half of all major reviews. And they're increasingly involved in many of the smaller reviews. Will your agency be included in a review if neither the prospective client nor the search consultant has heard of you? Not likely. Getting on the radar screen of search consultants is a fine art, because each search consultancy seems to have its own preferences for dealing with agencies.

Curiously, agency search consultants are one of the only audiences agencies deal with that actually cares about agency credentials. In fact, many of them go to great lengths to collect agency facts and figures and request that agencies complete custom questionnaires and update online databases. On the other hand, some simply toss agency credentials in the garbage. Some encourage agencies to regularly send samples of work and new campaigns, while others say it's simply too much to keep track of. Some are happy to get e-mail updates from agencies; others are annoyed by it. The only consistent rule in dealing with search consultants is that you must get to know each of them individually. Ask them how they prefer to work. Then do what you do when cultivating prospective clients: tailor your communications to the consultant's wants, needs, and issues.

What other audiences do winning agencies cultivate? Referral sources like media reps and production partners. Business partners like attorneys and CPAs. Influential sources like reporters and editors of business and trade publications. And of course, past clients who have moved onto other companies.

Customers

Who are the basic audiences you want to reach with your marketing efforts?

What is the prospect's experience with and attitudes toward the product category?

What is the prospect's experience with your product or service in particular?

What factors influence the purchase of your products or services?

Competition

From the target prospect's perspective, who or what is your primary competition?

What is your position in terms of market share?

What are the strengths and weaknesses of your chief competitors?

Distribution

What are your channels of distribution?

What kinds of sales aids are used by the company?

Sales

What are your current sales and how does that compare to past years?

What are your sales goals, both short and long-term?

Marketing Communications

What job should advertising perform for the company?

How should the advertising be measured (sales, leads, awareness, attitudes, preference)?

How are advertising budgets set?

What are your needs in other areas of marketing communications beyond advertising? (Sales literature, point of purchase, Internet marketing, direct marketing, etc.)

How do you handle public relations?

Research

Do you have any past or current research studies?

(Continued on next page)

What information gaps do you currently have that research could help fill?

Agency/Client Relationship

Why are you looking for a new agency?

How would you evaluate your past advertising and marketing programs?

What criteria did you use to select other agencies to talk to, including ours?

What roles will the new agency be expected to perform?

What do you see as our strengths and weaknesses compared to other agencies?

A year from now, how will you measure the success of the marketing program?

What forms of compensation do you prefer?

Who approves the advertising?

The New Business Presentation

When and where is the presentation for your account?

What type of room will be used (equipment available, seating arrangements, lighting)

Who will attend from your company?

Who will be the key decision makers and can we interview them in advance?

What are you looking for in our presentation and how will the agency be evaluated?

THEY HAVE THE COURAGE TO BE SELECTIVE

What's true in positioning is true in new business. Effectiveness requires sacrifice. You can't be good at everything and you can't go after everybody. Pursue the clients who want you for what you can do, not what you can't do. Seek relationships only with clients who want what you can deliver. Don't fake through weaknesses; capitalize on strengths.

Among service firms, agencies are the only ones desperate enough to pursue business on terms that other professions would consider ludicrous. What other business would agree to spend hundreds of hours and thousands of dollars on a competition for a client who wants your best strategic thinking and finished recommendations, even though:

- You don't know the budget.
- You don't know their objectives.
- You're not allowed to contact management.
- You don't know how much you'll make on the business.

Agencies should look at clients as seriously as clients look at agencies. "We've been accused of screening our clients, and I think that's true," says Martin Puris of the legendary Amarati & Puris. "The client/agency relationship truly is like a marriage. You're not going to spend long hours with someone you don't like just because they're going to pay you."[7] It's no coincidence that the agencies that could be described as pathologically picky about new clients are the ones with the best new business track records. They make a psychological commitment to the prospect, or they don't go after it at all.

THEY KNOW THAT NEW BUSINESS IS NOTHING LIKE OLD BUSINESS

There's a constructive axiom among agencies that are successful at new business: "Sell wants, deliver needs." This is a simple reminder that the objective in new business is not to help clients increase brand awareness and sales – the objective is to get the business.

The rules in new business are not the same as in old business. In old business you have a responsibility to tell it like it is, whether the client wants to hear it or not. In new business, you have to evaluate whether giving that kind of unvarnished advice will help you get the account. Because if you don't get the account, your advice won't make any difference anyway. Once you have the business, then you can recommend dismantling their entire marketing program if you think you must. But you've got to gain their confidence first, and that means getting the business first.

Don't fall into the trap of believing that you can treat a new client the same way you treat an old client. Old clients actually want you to argue with them for what you believe is right. Prospective clients don't know you or trust you or respect you well enough to do that. As a

Pursue clients who want you for what you can do, not what you can't do.

dating strategy, how do you think it would work to offer a helpful critique of your date on your first night out together?

The objective is not to show the client how smart you are, to convince them you're right, or even to make them like you – it's to gain their confidence. As Bill Phillips of Ogilvy & Mather used to say, "Earn their respect, and love will follow." In fact, respect is the key ingredient in "good chemistry," which is so often touted as the reason why one agency wins over another. Good chemistry is not just a result of being friendly, it's the result of helping clients *solve their problems* in a friendly way.

THEY KNOW THAT NEW BUSINESS SUCCESS IS A MATTER OF PERSISTENCE, NOT A MATTER OF LUCK

As most clients will tell you, most agencies have a sporadic, stop-and-start new business program. They form a new business team that meets a few times, drafts an impressive list of action items, and makes assignments to key agency people. Then a remarkable thing happens: nothing. Is this the fault of the agency president, the new business team, or the agency's clients, who keep the agency occupied with day-to-day work assignments?

The answer is all of the above. And none of the above. "The real problem is that most agencies have an episodic approach to new business," observes one of the leading search consultants. "They create one-off, fancy and expensive mailings. When nothing happens after the first mailing they look at the expense, wonder what's wrong with the prospect for not responding and usually abandon the effort." Beyond lack of a new business program and lack of a person responsible is just plain *lack of persistence.*

New business is like growing asparagus; the best time to start is five years ago. Landing the clients you really want takes not just months, but sometimes years – years of providing useful information, helpful thoughts, and interesting ideas. But realize that a relationship cannot be developed by talking about yourself. Imagine going on a date and talking only about yourself – your good qualities, your life history, and all the great things you have done. It's very likely this approach would *not* result in a second date.

Don't worry about selling the agency. Just build trust.

Clients aren't really interested in talking about the agency; they're interested in talking about themselves (so are we all). So use your contact opportunities to talk about their brand, their industry, their issues, their challenges, and their marketing. If you must, you can even talk about how your agency can help, but only as a last resort, because you're now back to talking about the agency again instead of the client.

Try this six-month experiment. Use new business communications as a chance to talk only about the prospect and never about the agency. You'll have to restrain your management team with iron chains, because it's the nature of an agency to constantly sell itself. But for one-half year, don't worry about selling the agency at all. And never, ever try to unsell other agencies. Just build *confidence* with your prospective client by showing them that you have their interests — not the agency's interests — at heart. And, as Winston Churchill encouraged his generals, "Never, never, never give up."

THEY PUT SUBSTANCE OVER STYLE

One of my early mentors once told me, "Son, our clients lead dull and dreary lives. Part of what they like about working with an agency is that it's a little piece of show business. When you make a new business presentation, put on a show. The agency that puts on the best show wins." Was he right?

I recall a headline in *Adweek* several years ago that read something like "How a Few Scribbles Won a Major Car Account." The article was about how Goodby Silverstein & Partners had prevailed over much larger competitors to win the Isuzu account — not by staging a slick multi-media presentation, but by covering a wall with butcher paper and using the entire two hours of the presentation to hand draw a timeline representing the history of cars in America.

The great agencies go out of their way to put substance ahead of style. Given limited time and money to spend on new business pitches, agencies should worry about substance first and style last. *What to say* more than how to say it.

BE PREPARED: AGENCY QUESTIONNAIRE TOPICS

To avoid reinventing the wheel each time you have an RFP come through the door, create written answers to the most common questions and keep them on file on the agency computer network.

Agency size
Offices
Agency ownership
Key agency staff members
Billings by media
Years in business
Agency organization
Agency history
Agency mission or vision
Agency services
Specialized services
Service approach
Key strengths and achievements
Creative philosophy
Strategic planning approach
Methods for measuring results
Media management
Use of media buying services
Pre- and post-testing of advertising
Work process and practices
Turn-around time
Secondary resources
Technological capabilities
Memberships and affiliations
Clients, billings, and length of relationship
Client references
Account gains and losses
Case histories
New business target categories
Minimum budget requirements
Conflict categories
Compensation practices
Profit target
Schedule of fees and hourly rates
Billings history
History of profitability
Cost accounting system
Credit rating
Banking and credit references
Media payment policies
Competitive bidding policy

I once paid a visit to an agency that was going after a national restaurant chain. They were clearly the underdog, not only because the competing agencies were all three times their size, but they were located about 2,000 miles from the client headquarters and the other agencies in the pitch were right in the client's same city. This agency invited me into their new business war room to see what they were doing to prepare for the presentation, and I was totally taken back by the sheer volume of ideas they had on the wall. The entire room was covered with ideas for TV spots, radio commercials, print ads, coupons, promotions, point of sale. The room was full of *substance*. No PowerPoint presentation, no interactive DVD, no dancing girls — just lots and lots of solutions to the client's problems. Guess which agency got the account?

THEY KNOW THAT PUBLICITY IS EARNED, NOT GRANTED

There's a very good reason why most agencies never show up in the national trade or business press. They simply don't try. They don't think they can, so they don't. And like other elements of their new business program, their agency publicity program is sporadic and inconsistent.

Is it realistic for smaller agencies to get national press? It happens all the time, but it's not a matter of serendipity. Like new business, it's usually the result of sheer perseverance. And like new business, it must be someone's job or else it will be a job that never gets done. A PR-savvy member of your staff must have the responsibility to get to know the editors and reporters of the major trade and business publications, regularly send your best work, announce new campaigns and new people, and assign topics for guest columns to your agency's best writers.

It's after you become proficient in the little stuff that the big stuff happens. For example, after years of doing a consistently good job at getting agency news and work published, a small but talented agency in the western U.S. decided they had finally built up a portfolio of work worthy of a feature in *Communication Arts* magazine. They had already succeeded in getting individual pieces of their work published in the magazine's Advertising Annual. And they had invested the time to get to know the editors by following up by phone on submitted work. So now it was time to invite themselves to visit the magazine's offices, meet with the editors personally, and show the agency's portfolio. Two years (and many mailings and phone calls) later, the agency got their feature.

THEY KNOW THAT ULTIMATELY THE BEST SOURCE OF NEW BUSINESS IS FROM CURRENT CLIENTS

It costs five times less to get new business from a current client than a new one. Yet precious few agencies concentrate enough time and resources on helping their current clients to grow. We are too quick to take the client's annual budget and assume there's no more money for anything. There is always more money for things that can *make* money.

Thinking intensely about how you can grow a current client's business is not only in the best interest of the agency, it's also in the best interest of the client. This is not a simple exercise in cross-selling agency services. As professional services veteran David Maister observes, "Cross-selling does little, if anything, for the client." It's not just about introducing an advertising client to the public relations department. This means the client now has two teams to manage – advertising and public relations – instead of one. Where's the advantage for the client? She might as well go out and hire the best PR firm she can find.[8]

The advantage to the client is the *integration* of advertising and public relations services. Maister believes that firms shouldn't be asking their people to sell other departments, but to look for ways for different departments to work together. "There is thus a critical distinction between traditional cross-selling and integrated selling," he notes, "where the client has a chance to receive extra value."

> In new business, the objective isn't to convince the client you're right; it's to get the business.

To provide additional *integrated* services to your client, gather your account team together and consider questions like:

1. What projects or activities could we recommend to this client that they haven't thought of?
2. Could we help in new areas – design, Internet marketing, etc.?
3. Can we help in recommending new products, new uses, or new markets?

4. Is the client doing an adequate job at point of sale? Communicating with dealers or distributors?
5. What could be done to improve the client's basic sales literature?
6. Could we recommend a tracking study to help the client track changes in awareness and attitudes?
7. Are we keeping up with field trips, store checks, or visits to competitors?
8. Are we making the effort to join client industry organizations and attend industry trade shows?
9. Can we do a more thorough job of preparing annual or quarterly marketing plans?
10. Would the client/agency team benefit from an off-site planning retreat?
11. What big projects have been put off that really need to be addressed in the client's best interest? What can we do to help them move forward?
12. Are there people within the client organization we need to meet or build a better relationship with?

And lest we forget, doing superb work for current clients is ultimately the best new business weapon you can have. Clients have a way of finding out who the really talented agencies are, and they're the ones that get invited to the dance. If you wonder why the same 12 agencies keep showing up in all the high-profile reviews, it's not just because they're hot, but because they're *good*. Your agency shouldn't just aspire to be that popular, but to be that good at your craft. And for that, there is no new business trick or shortcut.

What changes do you need to make to your systems and procedures to help bring your positioning to life?

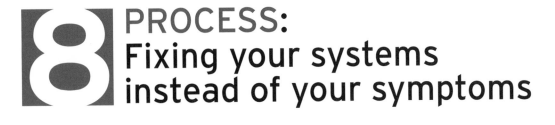

8 PROCESS:
Fixing your systems instead of your symptoms

FOR MOST AGENCY leaders, process isn't exactly their favorite subject. Which is precisely why process problems often top the list of complaints from the people in the agency who do the actual work. Process may not be an important ingredient of success in the role of a CEO, but it is imminently important to account managers who want to be successful in *their* role.

Think of process in terms of structure and systems — an architecture for getting things done.

Process — or lack of it — can make or break your branding strategy. It's where the rubber meets the road. So to make sure your process supports your positioning, consider each of the following questions.

1 Agency organization. *Does the agency need to be organized differently to allow us to deliver on our positioning?*

While a newly defined agency brand can sometimes mean that you need new people in new positions, it can also simply mean that you need to reorganize and redirect the people you already have. Not surprisingly, this often starts right at the top, where lack of definition of roles among partners creates organizational ripple effects felt throughout the entire agency.

To begin with, when an employee is asked to whom they report, the answer should not be "the partners." (An employee that is accountable to all of the partners isn't really accountable to any of them.) Can you image a foot soldier that has been told he reports not to his platoon leader, not to his commanding officer, not directly to a general, but to *all* the generals in his division? It wouldn't make for a very efficient army, and it doesn't make for a very effective agency.

The same blurring of responsibility occurs when partners resist defining their roles and insist on dabbling in everything from operations to finance, regardless of their particular area of expertise. So one of the first orders of business in aligning the agency organization behind the brand is to establish specific roles and responsibilities for each of the partners or principals. Then, based on each partner's role, establish direct reporting relationships.

AREAS OF PARTNER RESPONSIBILITY

Product
Brand planning
Research
Strategic planning
Creative
Production
Media
Interactive
Direct marketing
Public relations
Strategic alliances

People
Employee communications
Recruiting
Performance reviews
Employee compensation
Employee recognition program
Management team development
Training
New employee orientation
Policy and procedures

Promotion
Self-promotion materials
New business program
Publicity program
Agency marketing program

Process
Job processing system
Information retrieval
Financial management
Pricing agency services
Billing and cost accounting system
Compensation systems and agreements

Place
Workspace and environment
Office administration
Equipment and resources
Information technology

Beyond defining clearer roles and reporting relationships for the principals, the way the agency is branded may call for a wholesale reorganization of agency departments. This may mean the elimination of some departments and the creation of others. For example, in examining its core competencies and committing to a positioning, one agency decided that digital marketing was not a strength of the agency, so a division of several people was turned into a small department of one – essentially a digital marketing manager who coordinates the agency's interactive assignments with an outside provider.

Another agency decided that media planning was a core competency and an important component of the agency brand, but that media buying could be handled more efficiently by an outside media buying firm. So the media department was restructured to reflect the change.

In re-defining their brand, some progressive agencies take the issue of agency organization a step further by changing titles, flattening hierarchical structures, and assembling client-dedicated teams in place of departments. While some agencies have had impressive outcomes with this approach, the point is really to find the simplest structure you can to support your positioning, then make sure everyone's role in this structure is clearly understood – from the partners right on through to the runners.

2 Agency systems. *How do our agency systems or procedures need to change to be better aligned with our brand?*

Think about the recurring problems and crises you have in your agency. While your first reaction is likely to be "bad clients" or "bad employees," a lot of the difficulties you experience over and over again are actually caused not by bad people, but by bad systems. Veteran managers know that most "people problems" are actually "system problems."

Fixing broken systems, reconciling conflicting systems, and establishing needed new systems are all high-leverage activities for managers. To a large degree, the number of crises you confront each day is directly proportional to the lack or presence of good systems in your agency. A senior manager in an agency with good systems is able to focus on the work that really matters – serving the agency's clients. In an agency with bad systems, he or she would typically spend half the day dealing with workflow scheduling problems, half-baked strategic solutions, missed deadlines, and upset clients. Unless you're willing to spend a few days or weeks dealing with *systemic* problems, you'll experience months or years of *symptomatic* problems.

There is no greater fallacy in business than the idea that the way to create a laid-back environment is to take a laid-back approach to management. The only way you can create an environment in which employees are free to do the important *custom work* of the agency is if you have systems to take care of the *routine work*. Why should anyone have to stop and wonder about the best way to move a job through the agency? You'd be surprised how many do.

The fact that your staff complains about procedures is human nature. It's almost a sport, like criticizing politicians. Besides, who enjoys filling out timesheets and job orders? But if you want to hear the staff complain even louder, take the systems away. Even wild-at-heart agency types know that the quality of life is much better in a regulated civilized society than a lawless third-world country.

Unless you're willing to spend a few days or weeks dealing with systemic problems, you'll experience months or years of symptomatic problems.

Beyond having good basic systems, you need systems that allow you to deliver on your positioning. I once worked with an agency that had decided to reposition itself from a high-volume, high-output producer of below-the-line work to more of a strategically-minded provider of marketing solutions. (The first question you might ask is if this was a good idea, given their apparent core competencies in collateral production. But the members of this group had equally strong credentials in higher-level work that they brought from prior agencies.) To make the transition, they needed to dismantle and generally overhaul their entire approach to systems. They fundamentally moved from a business model of high-output/low added-value to low-output/high-added value. Some of the most important procedures the agency created to support this move were proprietary strategic planning and brand development systems. Because they were totally devoted to creating strong alignment between their desired positioning and their systems, the change produced almost immediate results. Within a year, they were named the leading agency in their region and achieved national notoriety with cover stories in the business press.

3 Project management. *How should we change the way jobs and assignments are processed through the agency?*

Without a doubt, the more your agency is oriented around high volume, high output work, the more critical effective project management is. It's intriguing, however, to observe how project management is the stepchild in some agencies and the star student in others. Like many things, it can be a direct reflection of the personalities of the agency principals.

Positioning or no positioning, effective project management is the unsung hero at countless profitable agencies, where it is treated like a respectable discipline in its own right. For example, agencies such as Lowe Roche in Toronto have canonized project management instead of treating it as a stepping stone to something better. There, "business managers" work as peers alongside "strategic planners," and have an opportunity to earn the same money and enjoy the same prestige.

Given the critical importance of delivering work on time and on budget, it only makes sense for agencies to do more to foster and reward those who are gifted in the areas of logistics, administration, and organization, just as they value those with strategic and creative smarts. A brilliant project manager can make as important a contribution to the success of a client relationship as a brilliant brand manager any day of the week.

> ## You cannot create a laid-back environment by taking a laid-back approach to management

4 Billing practices. *Do we need to change our rates, our billing practices, or our compensation systems to better reflect our desired brand?*

Given your agency positioning, are you charging enough for your services? Does the quality of work you're doing justify higher hourly rates? Should you be asking for bigger production budgets so you can produce higher quality work? Are you under priced for the markets you want to serve? The answers to these questions could be "yes" if you're moving away from serving local clients and seeking more regional or national business.

Similarly, your billing practices may have to migrate as well. While some smaller clients may be satisfied with a simple invoicing system, you may be taking your agency into markets where clients want and need a higher level of sophistication, including more detailed estimating, reconciling estimated costs with actual costs, and providing sometimes extensive backup documentation.

Even more than your billing system, your method of compensation can directly reflect on your agency brand. If you want to be seen as more of a counselor and less of an "agent," you should consider moving completely away from commissions in favor of fees. And if your business model is to demonstrate accountability in your client relationships, adopting some of the new incentive compensation systems is a powerful way to do it.

5 Financial information. *Do we need to change the way we track, report, and share financial information?*

If knowledge is power, it's no wonder why owners and managers of agencies have such supremacy. Top managers meet to pour over the numbers, but rarely provide the kind of financial information that would be helpful to individual employees and departments to help them improve their personal and group profitability.

The reluctance to share financial data can run deep in the cultural veins of an agency. Mostly, it is born out of fear that somehow employees will use the information to get the agency or its clients in trouble. But if you hold your people responsible for the profitability of clients and assignments, you must also give them the financial information they need to diagnose and correct problems.

KEY NUMBERS

Gross Income
Gross income generated

Operating Expenses
Percent of operating expenses to income
Percent of salary to gross income

Gross Profit
Profit before taxes

Productivity Indicators
Gross income per employee
Average percent billable time per employee
Average percent profit per client
Percent of gross income in cancelled time
  or charges

Surprisingly, sometimes even the most senior levels of management in an agency are unaware of key financial indicators. Information about billable time, cancelled charges, staffing expense, and direct expenses are crucial tools in running an agency with profitable people, profitable departments, and profitable clients.

No matter what your positioning, you can dramatically improve the odds of your business strategy's success by tracking a few "key numbers" and sharing them with your key staff members.

Of course some of the numbers in your organization need to remain confidential except at the most senior levels – information like salaries and bonuses. But you can easily segregate what ought to be shared with whom into three tiers:

	Principals	Senior Management Team	Staff
Key numbers (see above)	✔	✔	✔
Write-offs and cancelled charges	✔	✔	✔
Accounts receivable report	✔	✔	✔
Estimate variance report	✔	✔	✔
Income and expense forecasts	✔	✔	
Capital expenditures	✔	✔	
Budget variance report	✔	✔	
Income statement and balance sheet	✔		
Cash flow forecast	✔		
Raises and bonuses	✔		

The only way your people can be committed to the financial health of the agency is if they are involved in it. As the saying goes, "No involvement, no commitment."

6 Production efficiency. *Given our focus, do we need to work faster, or do we need more time?*

If your agency brand is focused around large, multiple-location retail clients, clearly you'd better have a job processing system that moves work through the agency at near warp speed. And a traffic system that can distribute it to far-flung locations at the speed of a satellite transmission.

AN INVENTORY OF AGENCY SYSTEMS

While not all of the following fit the traditional description of "system," looking at each of these topics as systems is useful in discovering if you have a shared approach to getting work done in the agency.

Product
Brand audit system
Brand development system
Strategic planning system
Creative development system
Print production system
Broadcast production system
Interactive production system
Competitive information collection system
Concept testing system
Legal review and clearance system
Media ordering system
Job processing system
Client records system
Client metrics measurement system
Client relationship evaluation system
New client start-up system
Brand review system

People
Recruiting system
Employment agreement system
New employee orientation system
Employee records system
Performance review system
Employee benefit administration system
Agency meeting system
Training systems
Employee termination system
Agency goal planning system
Management reporting system
Employee compensation system
Employee recognition and reward system
Administrative help system

Promotion
Prospective client identification system
New business database system
New business inquiry handling system
Marketing materials system

(Continued on next page)

For a firm oriented more toward design and brand identity, the implications are radically different. This kind of organization needs a production process that takes into account not just a longer set of timeframes, but a whole set of complex design issues having to do with special materials, specialized vendors, and special delivery and set up.

Unquestionably, the pressure from the client community to do things faster is relentless. And it's not just due to unreasonableness or lack of consideration on their part; more often it's because their own timeframes have been compressed through accelerated business planning, reactions to changing market conditions, and pressure to add to the bottom line, and fast. And while there is always the genuine emergency crash-and-burn assignment, the biggest mistake agencies make is to blindly accept unreasonable time frames.

If you ask different people in the same agency "How much time does the agency generally need to create and produce the average print ad?" the answers will vary from "two months" to "two weeks" to "two days." Many account executives honestly don't know the answer to this question, which is why they keep making irrational promises to clients. It will sound like an oversimplification to say that the solution is to publish standard production timetables, because timetables are routinely violated. However, that's just the point. Without a common standard, rush jobs become the rule instead of the exception.

7 Policies. *Are any of our policies in conflict with our positioning?*

Every businessperson knows from personal experience that there are two kinds of company policies: formal and informal. The formal policies are the ones published in the policy manual or employee handbook, and address such stirring subjects as vacation policy and health insurance. Actually, having such policies in writing is vital – if not practically, then legally.

But the policies that have the most impact in an agency are the informal, unwritten ones – the cultural norms that define how the agency really operates. The prime source of dissonance among employees is when the unstated norms contradict the stated aims of the agency. The best example is the agency that professes to prize originality, but caves in at the slightest objection from a conservative client. Pretty soon, the staff begins to understand that creativity isn't really something management believes in.

When you undertake the process of defining your agency's purpose, principles, and positioning, you've got to do some

Cold calling system
Agency mailing system
Agency publicity system
Award entries system
Directory listing system
Speaking program system
Search consultant marketing system
RFP development system
New business presentation development system
Work sample collection system
Agency Web site update system
Internet marketing system

Process
Income and expense forecasting system
Cash flow forecasting system
Budgeting system
Accounts payable system
Time collection system
Estimating system
Compensation system
Purchase order system
Billing system
Financial reporting system
Write off system
Past due collection system
Profit sharing system
Copyright and talent release system
Expense reimbursement system
Agency and client filing system

Place
Agency furniture and decorating system
Building security system
Emergency procedure system
Office supply system
Room and resource scheduling system
Intranet and extranet systems
Computer maintenance system
Internet security system
Telephone and voice mail system
Mail distribution system
Paging system
Library system
Subscriptions system
Shipping and delivery system
Storage system (on-property and off-site)
Disaster recovery system

serious soul-searching to make absolutely sure it's something you can really live with. While you should change what you can in your organization, you must also come to grips with the things you can't (or more to the point, won't) change. These are your deeply held cultural norms, and if you set your agency on a course that's in conflict with them, the entire process of defining an agency brand will leave you worse off than when you started. Aligning what you say with what you do is the only way you'll ever succeed in building a strong agency brand, and "what you say" must be aligned with both kinds of policies – written and unwritten.

HOW THE BEST AGENCIES DO IT

While every agency will always have its own way of doing things, there are some consistent characteristics of agencies that pay attention to process – and get better work as a result.

THEY REALIZE THAT NOT HAVING A SYSTEM IS STILL A SYSTEM

In their early years, some of the agencies with creative reputations seem to pride themselves on their lack of process (on the theory that process inhibits creativity), but sooner or later they come to the profound and uneasy realization that lack of process actually makes their jobs harder, not easier. Purposefully not having a system is still a system – just an agonizingly bad one.

My friend Jim Mountjoy, partner and creative director of the much-awarded Loeffler Ketchum Mountjoy, has a presentation he gives to ad clubs in which he draws a pyramid of success. At the base of that pyramid are the words "Operational Excellence" – this coming from a creative guy and a creative agency, both of which are supposed to be genetically opposed to systems. But over 20 years of experience crafting great ads has taught Jim that it actually takes a smooth-running agency to create, produce, and sell great creative work, the same way it takes a smooth running construction crew to build a great building.

Insisting on operational excellence is really the equivalent of the saying, "Give me the freedom of a tightly-defined creative brief." A well-defined process gives you freedom to think about the *problem* instead of thinking about the *process*.

THEY HAVE GIVEN A LOT OF THOUGHT TO PROCEDURES SO THEIR EMPLOYEES DON'T HAVE TO

It's tempting to adopt the point of view that because an advertising agency is a creative enterprise, systems and procedures should be kept to an absolute minimum. If you think about it, it could also be argued that precisely *because* an agency is a creative enterprise, it needs more systems more than a lot of other companies. The agency business is subjective enough in the first place. (How long does it take to have a good idea? How many days will you need to solve that problem? How much does it cost to produce a great television commercial?) So taking a subjective business and running it in a subjective way only makes things worse. It creates a world in which the ad gets done when it's done, the job costs what it costs, and the spot is ready to air when its ready. And clients fire agencies for ineptitude.

It is one of the essential jobs of management – even in a creative organization like an agency – to put into place good systems that allow good people to spend their time getting things done instead of trying to figure out *how* to get things done.

THEY KNOW THAT THE RECURRING CRISIS ISN'T A PROBLEM WITH PEOPLE, IT'S A PROBLEM WITH PROCESS

Are timesheets always late? Is billing always in a mess? Do jobs constantly come in over estimate? Any time you find yourself dealing with the same problem over and over again, it's usually a symptom not of bad people, but of bad process.

Another sure symptom of a company with bad systems is that they spend far too much of their time in meetings. And, as we all know, a company that meets all the time is a company that doesn't get anything done.

Again, a lot of agency principals *hate* dealing with systems and procedures. In fact, a lot of them simply refuse, because it's not something they enjoy or have any interest in. So their chronic problems stay chronic, just like a leaky tire. Meanwhile, the people on their staff that *do* care (and are affected most by bad systems) suffer.

There's another reason why some agency executives don't address process problems. Agency people like excitement. Some of them even enjoy a good daily crisis. To those who depend on solving urgent problems for their feelings of self-worth, a well-run agency can be a pretty dull place. Peter Druker tells about the difference between visiting a well-run manufacturing plant and a poorly managed one. "A well-managed factory is boring," he says. "Nothing exciting happens in it because the crises have been anticipated and have been converted into routine."[1]

Good systems allow good people to spend their time getting things done instead of trying to figure out how to get things done.

Agency managers who thrive on chaos have to decide which they value most: the efficiency and sanity of their staff, or feeding their irrational habit. If you're addicted to excitement, consider that there are other more positive and productive ways to inject interest into your day (like helping your clients develop some ground-breaking marketing ideas.)

If you want to reduce the number of times the bell rings in the firehouse, fix your systems, not your symptoms.

THEY STREAMLINE SYSTEMS SO THEY CAN SPEND TIME ON CLIENT BUSINESS

Interviews of agency staffers reveal that one of the most common complaints is, "Everyone seems to have their own way of doing things." It's not that the agency doesn't have a system. It's that it has 52 of them.

So instead of spending time figuring out client problems, agency people are trying to figure out agency systems. Imagine a factory with no clear system for transforming raw materials into finished products. Agencies are factories for ideas. And while the process for developing solutions to marketing problems can never be as predicable as an assembly line, everyone in the agency should have the same understanding of what it takes to make the agency's finished product.

Streamlining systems and processes allows the agency's greatest asset — its people — to provide the value they were hired for in the first place.

In the final analysis, all processes either make you money or cost you money.[2] Good systems increase the profitability of your agency by increasing the productivity of your people. Bad systems sap not only productivity, but energy and enthusiasm. As a manager, you really can't afford to be neutral on the subject.

What changes do we need to make in the area of facilities and resources to help bring our positioning to life?

PLACE:
Putting The Style
Behind The Substance

THE RECEPTION AREA of Agency A has mismatched furniture, a broken chair in the corner, and a coffee table with a disheveled stack of magazines dating from 1986. Plaques and awards are nailed haphazardly on surrounding walls. And the receptionist is nowhere to be found.

Agency B presents quite a different impression. It happens to be an agency that is positioned around outdoor adventure. It has a climbing wall behind the reception desk. Instead of a coat closet, it has a row of lockers. And in addition to its logo on the wall, it has the words "Let's have fun" painted in giant letters.

BASIC TOUCH POINTS OF AN AGENCY BRAND

Agency Identity
Name
Logo standards
Typographical standards
Color standards

Telephone
How telephone is answered
How calls are handled
Music (or commercials) on hold
Company and individual voice mail greetings

Lobbies
Signage
Décor and furnishings
Organization and cleanliness
Display of work and awards
Reading materials

Offices
Décor and furnishings
Organization and cleanliness
Nameplates

Meeting Rooms
Décor and furnishings
Organization and cleanliness
Writing pads and pens
Accessories for meal and coffee service

Communication
E-mail messages (electronic stationery)
Letters, memos, and faxes
Conference and Status reports
Plans and recommendations
Billing statements
Agency intranet
Extranets (used for client communication)
FTP site

Presentations
Leave-behinds
PowerPoint format
Board design

Promotion
Web site
Downloadable agency brochure
Agency DVD

As the saying goes, "If you want to play the part, you have to look the part." The look of the agency is the most obvious manifestation of the importance of "place" in building the agency brand, but place is really concerned with several different dimensions.

1 **Offices.** *What does our place of business say about the agency brand?*

As TBWA/Chiat/Day's Lee Clow says, "Nothing kills the spirit faster than dead offices." The agency that created the admired "think different" campaign for Apple Computer also tries to work different. Their creation of an eclectic "advertising city" reinforces their credo: Change the rules. Among other things, the agency also has a pirate's skull and crossbones painted on the center of a basketball court. "If you stay focused on the environment as a celebration of what the agency believes in and does," says Clow, "it can become a kind of manifestation of the spirit of the company."[1]

Walk into any office of Ogilvy & Mather and you'll see red. Their logo is red, the brochures on the coffee table are red, sometimes even the walls or carpet is red. This motif stems from David Ogilvy's famed red braces, which he wore as a personal trademark. Ogilvy believed that the quality of the agency offices was a direct reflection of the quality of the agency:

"The physical appearance of our offices is important, because it says so much about Ogilvy & Mather. If they are decorated in bad taste, we are yahoos. If they look old-fashioned, we are fuddy-duddies. If they are too pretentious, we are stuffed shirts. If they are untidy, we are inefficient. Our offices must look efficient, contemporary, cheerful, and functional."[2]

At Ogilvy & Mather headquarters in New York, even the security guards reflect the brand. They wear a black suit and gray sweater (rather than the standard-issue blue security uniform) as a statement that the O&M brand is a cut above.

In office appearance, there is always a balance to strike. Ostentatious display makes clients assume they're being overcharged. Spartan environments make clients fear they're dealing with losers or beginners. An associate of mine, Steve Cuno, who runs a direct response agency called Response Advertising, was surprised at the effect his spiffy but tasteful new offices had on clients and prospects, who seemed suddenly a little more proud to associate with the agency. "Better surroundings also lifted moral of the staff," says Steve. "The effect says as much about the rightness of our new surroundings as it does about the wrongness of our old ones."

2 First impressions. *Are we sending the right message about our brand when others make contact with us?*

What is the first impression most people have of the agency? Very often it's the way they are greeted or treated on the phone. Do you have a receptionist, or do calls go directly into a pre-recorded voice mail system? If you have a human answering the phone, is he or she pleasant, polite, and articulate? Does this person say, "Yeah hang on a minute," or "Just a moment please? (You'd be surprised how many receptionists create a less-than-stellar first impression of your agency by being either unpleasant or unhelpful.) One agency, LLKFB in New York, rewarded a particu-

HOW ONE AGENCY DID IT

Instead of making their place of business an afterthought, one forward-looking agency outlined and accomplished an ambitious set of brand alignment initiatives. Here were some of the items on their list:

- Put new signage in lobby
- Build a war room
- Install T-1 line for faster Internet access
- New digital projector and ceiling screen for conference room
- New digital copiers
- Improve employee parking
- Organize and update file server room
- Establish central library for periodicals
- Supply the reception area with coffee, soda, and reading materials

larly talented receptionist and underscored the importance of making a good first impression on visitors and callers by giving her the title "Director of First Impressions."

At your agency, when calls are put on hold, does the call go into a black hole of silence or do you use this as an opportunity to reinforce your agency brand? If you have the good fortune to be put on hold when calling the offices of RiechesBaird in southern California, you'll enjoy a few snippets of tunes from old TV shows. And if you have the opportunity to visit their well-designed offices, you'll be reminded a little bit of Toon Town in nearby Disneyland.

Everything about the way the agency looks, feels, and sounds should reflect the agency brand.

What do visitors see when they first step into your reception area? Is it stylish or sterile? Does your lobby feel like Dilbertland, with a modular furniture desk, a blank white wall, and standard issue visitors chairs? What does it say about your agency brand when you have a pool table in the entrance, like the offices of a notable San Diego agency?

A West Coast shop wanted to create a leading-edge impression by constantly running the agency's television work on a huge plasma screen in the front lobby. The impression of a "connected" agency is reinforced by video conferencing capabilities in every conference room, a high-tech "central intelligence" market research area, and "brand war rooms" with dedicated computers, monitors, projectors, and screens throughout the agency.

The agency brand is manifest in multiple touch points, both inherent and created. Virtually all of them can be proactively managed to create the kind of experience that will add strength to the brand. Some are obvious, but that's all the more reason not to overlook them.

3 Working environment. *Do our furnishings and equipment help us to be at our best?*

When you visit the open offices of Weiden & Kennedy in Portland, it's pretty clear you've stepped onto the premises of a collaborative organization. The eclectic Mad Dogs & Englishmen in New York makes their integrated style even more explicit with moveable workstations instead of traditional stationery desks. A flexible-thinking L.A. agency keeps their offices completely modular with what they call "Walls on Wheels," which allows them to create offices or war rooms at will. At the Richards Group in Dallas, founder Stan Richards designed an agency in which he can stand on a balcony and address the entire agency, assembled on staircases. A successful agency in the southwestern U.S. has a huge central area called "Town Center" in which the entire agency can be assembled for meetings, parties, and presentations.

HOW EMPLOYEES FEEL ABOUT THEIR PLACE OF BUSINESS

Very often, agency managers are unaware of just how much the business environment affects employees. In a recent internal survey, a small agency with a reputation for great work learned that it had a soft underbelly when it came to "place" issues. Here are some actual written employee responses to a question about agency weaknesses:

"Antiquation of general systems, bad phones, very bad computers, no systems in place. I'm not one for 'systems,' but as we grow we need organization."

"Lack of organized systems, horrible technology, bad space planning and internal materials organization, too much reliance on ineffective office management, desire to stay 'homey,' location (ugly building, bad parking, busy area, cramped quarters, seems cheap and cheesy)."

"Not having the structure, supplies and resources that I think are pretty basic is a big weakness."

While every agency has its own style and culture, in many shops the working environment is too much like a bank and not enough like an energetic creative enterprise. The point is to be deliberate about the way your offices look. Develop and apply a decorating standard for your agency brand. This is no job for amateurs. For office build outs you need a good architect, and for office décor you need a good interior designer. Resist the temptation to do it yourself for the same reasons you would advise a company not to do their own advertising. Hiring a professional can also help avoid the internal squabbles about what color to paint the walls or how to decorate the conference room. Invest your confidence in professional architects and designers who understand what you're trying to accomplish with you agency brand; then let them do their jobs.

Take an active interest in the kinds of furnishings and equipment you have provided to your rank and file employees. It's often embarrassing to see the office of the CEO

THE VIRTUAL OFFICE

Because your intranet is a virtual office or place of business, it can be a huge reinforcement and advocate of the agency brand. Same for extranets you can develop for interfacing with clients. Here are a few things to consider.

Agency Intranet
- E-Mail
  - By department
  - By person
- Lists
  - Employee list and contact information
  - Phone extension list
  - Employee birthdays
  - Office holidays
- Clients
  - Client contact information
- Job Processing
  - Job number catalog
  - Job order
  - Purchase order
  - Production timetables
- Office Forms
  - Memo
  - Expense report
  - Timesheet
  - Vacation request form
  - Cash advance request
- Agency Promotional Materials
  - Bios
  - Case histories
  - Client references
- Proposals
  - Questionnaire responses
  - New business proposals
- Business Partners
  - Production partners
  - Media partners
  - Other business partners
- News
  - New people
  - News clips
- Support
  - Computer support
  - Office machines

(Continued on next page)

furnished in 18th century antiques while account executives work in Spartan cubicles with threadbare chairs and a total lack of creature comforts. Would you enjoy working in an environment like that? Your people don't either.

4 Tools and resources. *Have we armed our people with the things they need to do their best work?*

An agency positioned in the realm of travel and tourism will likely be a member of the Travel Industry Association, subscribe to *Travel Weekly*, get daily e-mail updates of travel news with *Travel Advance,* and attend the World Travel Market show. They will also have access to proprietary travel-related databases and research studies. In short, they will have all the tools and resources to make them experts in their field.

Some agencies suffer from some very simple resource problems, from broken desk chairs to lack of basic office supplies. Lest you be tempted to think this couldn't apply to you, talk to a few of your people. When it comes to resources, most agencies have a few blind spots. I once visited an agency where they kept running out of copy paper. No one in the agency was assigned to order it. What seems like a minor thing was actually a major problem.

In one agency survey after another, one of the chief sources of employee frustration is slow and outmoded computers. This is because the IT department has supplied the top executives with state of the art technology, while assistant media planners are working with hand-me-downs from 1992. The computer is now such an integral part of business life, to be saddled with a sluggish or uncooperative machine is painful if not downright maddening. The same goes for old versions of operating systems or other software. Agencies that are well equipped and well organized in the area of technology have vastly happier, more productive employees. But very often, the chief executive must take a personal interest to make sure everyone in the agency has the tools they need to do their jobs.

- Building security
- Ordering supplies

Information Resources
- Web site subscription information
- Industry library access
- Etc.

Financial
- Chart of hourly rates
- Client compensation agreements

Employee Handbook
Job Openings
Employee Bulletin Board

Client Extranets
Estimates
Invoices
Create works
Conference reports
Status reports
Results
Media schedules
Creative briefs
Marketing plans
Budgets

In business, as in life, sometimes the small things are the big things. If you don't believe it, take an anonymous survey of your employees on the subject and you'll quickly learn how crummy parking, outdated office equipment, and sloppy office organization send an unspoken message about how much management cares (or doesn't care) about the day-to-day contentment of its people. As the great architect Frank Lloyd Wright said, "If you give men and women some dignity and pride in their environment, it all comes out to the good where the product is concerned."

When it comes to thinking about "place," you have to take a deliberate look at both style and substance. Remember that the agency brand is more than skin deep. Of course, everything about the way the agency looks, feels, and sounds should reflect the agency brand. But be-neath the surface, the agency and its people must have the tools and resources to back it all up.

BRINGING THE AGENCY BRAND TO LIFE

What matters most (and what matters least) in bringing your positioning to life?

10 PRIORITIES:
If Everything Is Important, Nothing Is Important

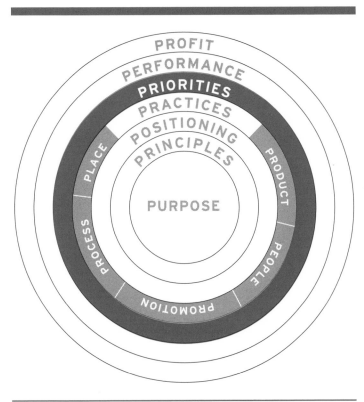

ON THE BATTLE-FIELD, doctors use the art and science of triage: they separate the wounded into three categories. The first category is people who are going to live, with or without medical treatment. The second category is people who are going to die, with or without treatment. The third category is people who will die unless they get treatment. It's this last category that gets the priority treatment.[1]

With the numerous agency branding initiatives staring you in the face, setting priorities is a crucial step on the pathway to success. This is the art of "first things first." If you try to put *everything* first, everyone – including you – will become discouraged.

HOW ONE AGENCY TOOK THE INITIATIVE ON INITIATIVES

After a series of agency audits and employee interviews, one agency prioritized their branding initiatives this way.

Product Initiatives

1. Develop a propriety strategic planning process that's more relevant to clients who match our positioning.
2. Establish a better account planning capability.
3. Cultivate new outside resources for direct marketing, marketing research, and high-end graphic design.
4. Develop extranets for major clients to facilitate communication and make it easy for clients to interface with our agency brand.
5. Establish a new model for integrating interactive marketing into the rest of the agency.

People Initiatives

1. Define hiring standards that are compatible with our positioning, including an interview guide.
2. Revise the new employee orientation program to include indoctrination about our branding strategy.
3. Develop a better approach to performance reviews based on desired behaviors that support the agency brand.
4. Devise a training program to teach employees about their role in achieving the agency's branding strategy.
5. Develop an employee recognition program that rewards behavior consistent with the agency brand.

Promotion Initiatives

1. Based on our new positioning, develop a creative brief for the agency as a brand.
2. Revise our corporate identity materials to better reflect our brand.
3. Update the promotional materials and the Web site to showcase key elements of the agency brand.

(Continued on next page)

Unless you do something radical, the pressures of daily agency life will always win over the priorities required to re-brand the agency. That's question is, which will win – the important priorities or the everyday demands?

WHAT'S MOST IMPORTANT?

Ask yourself "What difference would a clear vision of our purpose, principles, and positioning make in the way we prioritize and spend our time?" If you have done the work to define your purpose, principles, and positioning, you now have the guide-posts to help define your priorities. Purpose, principles, and positioning become the compelling impetus behind every decision you make. They provide the deep burning "yes" that empowers you to say "no" to the less important things. As Stephen Covey says, "Anything less than a conscious commitment to the important is an unconscious commitment to the unimportant."[2]

The main thing is to keep the main thing the main thing.

GETTING TEAMS TO SPEARHEAD YOUR INITIATIVES

No agency leader can do all this alone. You need the energy, talent, and commitment of your key people to bring your agency brand to life. You need a coalition of your top people who are committed to the agency brand and willing to lead the charge into new territory. You can't have commitment from half your teams and complacency from the others.

Aligning your practices with your positioning should be the responsibility of a select group of agency management and staff, organized into "alignment teams." These teams should have representatives from different functions within the agency. Members must also be selected for their proactivity, their talents, and their interest in the agency's success – the people who speak up in staff meeting and come to you occasionally with ideas to improve the agency.

Caution: Never, ever assign team members based solely on a feeling of obligation or because you believe they should be on the team by virtue of their position or tenure with the agency. If you do, nothing will ever get done and cynicism for your branding revolution will quickly set in. Select members based on their ability to contribute and their willingness and ability to work outside their regular daily responsibilities – and nothing else.

You'll need five task teams, each consisting of no more than five people. It will be their job to:

4. Refine the agency's new business database based on more selective criteria for new clients.
5. Step up the agency publicity program and make news with our new positioning.

Process Initiatives

1. Improve and standardize our job processing system and give our teams better access to job-related information.
2. Replace our current agency software system with one that will provide real-time on-line information sharing.
3. Create additional income categories in our billing system for new areas of service established as part of the agency rebranding.
4. Explore better ways to be compensated by clients for the investment the agency makes in specialized hardware and software required to support our brand.
5. Do a better job of providing regular profitability and productivity reports to members of the management team.

Place Initiatives

1. Redecorate and update the look of the agency to reflect our branding strategy.
2. Provide employees with upgraded technology resources, home access to agency e-mail and network files.
3. Display our best work more conspicuously in well-traveled areas of the agency, with an emphasis on work that reflects our new agency focus.
4. Replace worn-out and outdated furnishings that reflect poorly on our desired brand image.
5. Equip our meeting rooms with branded accessories (writing materials, coffee and food service, etc.) that show we take pride in our brand.

1. Identify the needed initiatives in each of the five major areas of agency practices (product, people, promotion, process, and place).

2. Realistically prioritize the list of initiatives in each practice area.
3. Design an action plan to carry out the initiatives.
4. Recruit help from other agency members to execute the initiatives.
5. Regularly monitor the success of the initiatives and report to management.

Let's take a look at how task teams can tackle each of these areas of responsibility.

1 Identify the needed initiatives *in each of the five major areas of agency practices.*

In the course of defining your agency brand, you have no doubt started to make a fairly significant list of specific strategies needed to achieve your vision. Now is the time to form your alignment teams and let them add to, sift through, and prioritize the list. Here are some of the subjects each team will need to consider in each practice area:

Product Task Team
- Agency services, capabilities and disciplines
- Account assignments and approach to client service
- Integration of agency departments and capabilities
- Approach to strategic and creative development
- Client compensation systems
- Suppliers, business partners and strategic alliances
- Information resources
- Communication with clients
- Association memberships and networking

People Task Team
- Agency organization
- Management team structure
- Roles, responsibilities, and job descriptions
- Training and professional development
- New employee orientation
- Agency meetings and company events
- Internal communication
- Hiring and recruiting standards and practices

- Performance review process
- Agency policies

Promotion Task Team

- Corporate identity
- New business program
- Criteria for prospective clients, new business list and prioritization
- Agency credentials and promotional materials
- Agency marketing program
- Search firm relationships and networking with referral sources
- Agency publicity program

Process Task Team

- Basic systems and procedures
- Job processing and workflow management
- Internal forms and formats
- Billing practices
- Cost accounting and financial information sharing system

Place Task Team

- First impressions (reception area, telephone greeting, lobby displays)
- Offices and facilities
- Agency décor
- Working environment
- Furnishings and equipment
- Technology tools and resources

2 Realistically prioritize the list of initiatives *in each practice area.*

Chances are, your list of initiatives is unrealistically long. Working with your task teams, shave the list down to *no more than five initiatives in each practice area.* This isn't to say that you're going to completely ignore all the other initiatives on your list; you're just going to put them on the back burner so you can focus on the most important matters first.

How do you select the top five initiatives in each area? Ask each team to make the evaluation based on these three key questions:

Which of these initiatives will make the most difference in helping us align our positioning with our practices?

It goes without saying that you should select priorities that help the agency walk its talk. These are the initiatives that help you *be* what you say. If you say you are a firm that specializes in customer relationship management but you lack some key aspects of database management, this should be a top "product" priority. If you have persons on staff who don't have the specific skills they need to deliver on your positioning, a professional development program would be a chief "people" priority. If you want a reputation as a leading-edge institution but the agency looks like it was last redecorated in 1957, you have some vital "place" initiatives that deserve priority attention.

The main thing is to keep the main thing the main thing.

Which of these initiatives will allow us to build on our strengths?

When it comes to selecting initiatives, it's only natural to select your biggest problems instead of your biggest opportunities. But this is almost always a mistake. Play to your strengths instead of trying to fix your chronic weaknesses. By focusing on what you can do (but need to do better) rather than what you can't do, you'll not only produce healthier results, you'll nurture team confidence. One success will lead to another.

The very worst thing you can do is select initiatives that are too big, too ambitious, and too difficult. The priorities you select must not be pipe dreams. It's OK if they make you stretch, but they must also be realistic. In fact, your approach to choosing and executing initiatives could be thought of as what business leader Larry Bossidy calls "the relentless pursuit of reality."[3]

Which of these initiatives will allow us to show immediate short-term results?

To start out, it's critical to select initiatives that you know you can accomplish in the short term. For one thing, it will give your task teams a taste of success. It will also demonstrate to the rest of the agency staff that progress is being made, and that the agency is changing. And it gives your team the confidence to tackle other, more challenging initiatives in the future.

3 Design an action plan *to carry out the initiatives.*

Ask the leader of each task team to develop a plan of action for accomplishing their respective initiatives. This should be a written document that answers the questions:

- **What**
- **Who**
- **When**

This must be updated on a regular basis and distributed both to the team members and the principals of the agency. The success of your branding initiatives depends on establishing roles, responsibilities, and due dates. In other words, accountability.

4 Recruit help from other agency members *to execute the initiatives.*

While the task team in charge of product has the responsibility for making sure product initiatives are accomplished, they're going to need the involvement and cooperation of a lot of people along the way. Brands are built from the inside out, and getting the participation of staff members at all levels is the only way to ensure that what you say on the outside is matched by what you do on the inside.

You not only need the help of the staff, you need their buy-in. If employees view these initiatives from afar, they will consider what you're doing your business – but not theirs. The changes you're making in the agency may start from the top, but you need top-to-bottom commitment to accomplish them.

Success comes as a result of making the time, not finding it.

5 Regularly monitor the success of the initiatives *and report to management.*

Your task teams will need mechanisms to keep the initiatives moving forward. Using a regularly updated action plan (what, who and when), each team should meet regularly to thrash out next steps, discuss barriers to success, and identify needed help and resources.

These must be regularly scheduled meetings, not get-togethers that happen when team members have time. They will never have the time, and they will never accomplish the initiatives if they simply try to fit them into their regular daily schedule. Success comes as a result of making the time, not finding it

When it comes to setting priorities, the worst thing you can do is *not* to decide. Or to decide only to change your mind a few weeks later. The staff soon learns that these aren't really priorities after all – just another brief foray into the next Idea of the Month. Or as an agency friend of mine says, "If you want to demoralize people, give them a moving target."

You have to match what you say on the outside with what you do on the inside.

I have observed many agency principles agree to a set of initiatives only to lose interest, faith, or focus a few weeks later. This is fatal. The leaders of the organization must set the example. If it's not important to you, you can be sure it will not be important to your staff.

Once organizational priorities have been determined, they must then become *personal* priorities or they will be only as valuable as the paper they're written on. Team members must have the discipline to organize their time in a way that allows them to work on key agency initiatives. Unless individual team members make a conscious decision to devote time to working on initiatives, the constant rush of client demands and deadlines will constantly overwhelm them.

If you and your task teams go about business as usual, it's very likely that your most vital initiatives won't get done at all. There are always more tasks to do in a given day than there are hours to accomplish them. So the goal simply can't be to get everything done; the goal is to decide which things are most important.

As Peter Drucker observes, work is traditionally focused on doing things right, but you should first focus on doing the *right* things. "Do first things first, and second things not at all," he counsels. "The alternative is to get nothing important done."[4]

Prioritizing your initiatives is essential. Otherwise, you risk getting trapped in "the thick of thin things." If everything is important, then nothing is important. Decide what to do – and what not to do – and turn your energies to the initiatives that will make the most difference. When you have achieved success with your first round of priorities, you can move onto the next round. With patience and persistence, you'll see dramatic results and changes in each practice area – product, people, promotion, process, and place.

How do you get your entire organization involved in executing your initiatives?

11 | PERFORMANCE:
The Job Of The
Executive Is To Execute

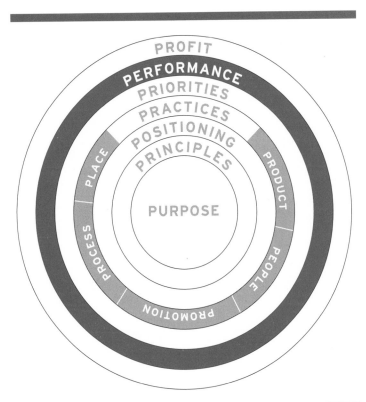

LET'S ASSUME BY now your agency has identified its purpose, principles and positioning. You have developed and prioritized key initiatives in each area of agency practice – product, people, promotion, process, and place. You have put teams into place and given them the responsibility to carry out the initiatives. You're now at a point where everything depends on *performance*. This is where you must now walk the walk.

Creating alignment between your positioning and your practices isn't just an important thing; it's the *only* thing. Unless you actually put your initiatives into action, nothing will have been accomplished. In the final analysis, the real difference between mediocre agencies and great ones is not vision, but execution. Nobody says it better than the groundbreaking thinkers on the subject, Jim Collins and Jerry Porras:

"Building a visionary company requires 1% vision and 99% alignment…the authenticity, the discipline, and the consistency with which the ideology is lived – not the content of the ideology – differentiate visionary companies from the rest of the pack."[1]

For most companies, the problem is not ideation; it's execution. We're too busy working on yesterday's problems to be able to work on tomorrow's initiatives.

This chronic challenge can produce persistent cynicism. Employees begin to mumble, "Yeah, we talk about a lot of things, but we never actually do any of them." Management talks up new initiatives but nothing really ever seems to change. The result is lost credibility, lost opportunity, and lost enthusiasm. And the agency CEO risks becoming the boy – or girl – who cried wolf.

TALK IS CHEAP, BUT EXECUTION IS PRICELESS

Too many agencies are more obsessed with how they look than how they *are*. A brand must not only say, it must *be*. The most important part of branding – the *being* – comes from the inside out. "The key failure for any company attempting to effect a gear change in its own performance," says Adam Morgan, "is not the ability to define its intention, but the inability to translate intention into behavior." In fact, Morgan believes it is not just commitment that is necessary to effect change, but overcommitment.[2]

There's a story about five frogs sitting on a log. One decided to jump. How many frogs were left? Five.

There's quite a difference between making the decision to jump and actually jumping. Many agencies make the decision to change. But only a few transform their decision into action.

Unless and until you translate your initiatives into action, the initiatives are really only intentions. Based on his years of observing the behavior of companies like ad agencies, consultant David Maister agrees. "A professional firm's values, standards, and indeed strategy are not defined by what the firm says it aspires to," says Maister, "but by what it is prepared to enforce."[3]

Talk isn't really cheap – it's expensive. Think of the countless hours wasted talking about the same issues over and over again.

As Stanford professor Jeffrey Pfeffer points out, "Companies often confuse talking with doing. They think talking about doing something is the same thing as doing it. That planning is the same thing as doing. That giving presentations is the same as doing. That making reports is the same as doing. Or even that making a decision to do something is the same thing as doing it."[4] Only doing is doing.

YOU CAN IF YOU THINK YOU CAN

The success you achieve in fulfilling your initiatives can be a self-fulfilling prophecy. If you think you can, you can. If you think you can't, you can't. Your staff knows where you stand, whether you verbalize it or not.

In effect, you'll get the results you expect. If you're doubtful and dubious, your staff will give only a half-hearted effort. But if you make it clear – by what you say as well as what you do – that you believe your initiatives are achievable, your staff will likely rise to the occasion.

> **Until you translate your initiatives into action, they are really only intentions.**

Business schools have reams of research showing the effect of management's expectations on the performance of employees. If you have high expectations, you get high performance. If you have low expectations, you might as well forget about anything changing. "It is as though there were a law that caused subordinates' performance to rise or fall to meet managers' expectations," observes a noted business school scholar who has written extensively on the subject. The powerful influence of a leader's expectations on staff performance means that more often than not, your people will do what they are expected to do.[5] You must first expect success in order to achieve success.

In the landmark book that practically defined the modern corporation, *The Practice of Management,* Peter Drucker argues that nothing motivates high performance as much as believing in and expecting high performance. Focusing a person's vision on an extraordinary goal produces extraordinary performance. On the other hand, to concentrate on the minimum required doesn't help either the person or the company. It only destroys a person's motivation.[6] High expectations centered around a goal that takes unusual effort produces unusual results. Normal expectations centered around a goal that takes the usual effort produces the usual results.

IF EVERYONE IS RESPONSIBLE, THEN NO ONE IS RESPONSIBLE

How many times have you attended a meeting that resulted in a lot of decisions, but no assignments? So were decisions really made?

If everyone in the room unanimously agrees that a particular action needs to be carried out, but no specific individual is given primary responsibility, what's the likely outcome? Probably another meeting in which the group agrees, "Yeah, we need to work on that." But who exactly is "we?" If "we" is assigned to a task it likely will never get done.

Without specific assignments and responsibilities, most "decisions" are really nothing more than good intentions.

ASSIGNING BOTH RIGHTS AND RESPONSIBILITIES

It's a lot easier to give responsibilities than it is to give rights. So many agency managers give the former but not the latter, and then wonder why nothing ever gets done. It takes courage to give rights. Who knows what disaster may befall the agency if you invest the rank-and-file with actual authority?

Delegating rights along with responsibilities creates some responsibilities for you, too. Like giving proper training and being hyper-clear about expectations. Then be prepared to be fair when employees take the ball, run with it, and stumble. It's certain that someone learning a new role will make a few mistakes. But they're just small mistakes compared to the big ones agency managers make. (As Bill Bernbach wisely observed, "The great mistakes are made when we feel we are beyond questioning."[7]) Furthermore, being given authority makes your people feel trusted and empowered.

Before you give someone the responsibility for a particular agency initiative, make sure you're willing to give her the accompanying authority — then get the heck out of the way. As David Ogilvy used to ask, "Why have a dog and do all of the barking yourself?"

SEEING PAST THE SHORT TERM

Agencies assure their clients that the real benefits of building a brand are long term. The same phenomenon holds true when building an agency brand. You can compare the process of building a great brand with going to the gym. If you look only at the short term, it can appear to be all pain and no gain. You and your staff spend time working on things that produce no apparent short-term result. But, like going to the gym, the results begin to show over time. If brands (including agency brands) want to become strong and healthy, they need to keep going to the gym.[8]

If a musician gave up on a difficult piece because she wasn't willing to practice, she would never become great. The fact is great musicians spend a lot of time practicing and relatively little time performing. Business people are just the opposite. Because we don't practice, we just recycle our problems. Even an accomplished musician has trouble playing a challenging score unless she keeps working at it. Accomplished executives need to invest the same time and effort before they can expect flawless performance of their initiatives. Change is, after all, a process – not an event.[9]

There simply is no shortcut, no quick fix. If the music or gym analogy makes you sweat, think of gardening. When it comes to building a great agency brand, you've got to plant and cultivate before you can harvest. If you don't plant, you can't harvest. You can't reap what you don't sow. At the end of the season, what you and your team produce will be a direct result of how willing you are to get your hands dirty.

WHY YOU MUST BE PERSONALLY COMMITTED AND INVOLVED

When Julius Caesar landed his Roman legions on the shores of the Dover Cliffs, he wanted to make sure his troops were fully committed to battling the tribes of fearsome Celts. He wanted to ensure performance. So as the legions made camp along the tops of the cliffs and prepared for war, they looked down to the water and saw something very motivating: Caesar had set fire to the entire fleet of Roman ships.

Execution will occur in an organization to the extent that the leader is personally committed. Until and unless the leader demonstrates personal involvement, the staff is unlikely to take change initiatives seriously. The stronger the personality of the leader, the more this is true. In agencies with a strongly opinionated CEO, the *only* things that get attention are the things the CEO personally cares about. As the inspirational leader of Herman Miller once said, "Our companies can never be anything we don't want ourselves to be."[10]

Agency leaders and managers can't delegate their responsibility for personal involvement in executing the company's initiatives. They can't have the attitude that execution and tactics are for administrative people. "Many people regard execution as detail work that's beneath the dignity of a business leader," observe the authors of *Execution,* one of the best books on the subject. "That's wrong. To the contrary, it's a leader's most important job." What's more, they believe that a leader's ultimate success isn't a result of strategy, but *execution.* "Do great CEOs and Nobel Prize winners achieve their glory through execution?" they ask. "Well, yes, in fact, and therein lies the grand fallacy." Nobody has ever achieved greatness without results.[11]

Execution will occur in the agency to the extent that the leader is personally committed.

Jack Welch left a legacy at GE not because he was a great visionary, but because he was a great executor. Business strategies at GE worked not just because they were well conceived, but because they were well executed. Welch performed, and he knew how to get his people to perform.

Some agency heads seem to practice management by abdication. With their doors closed and their heads planted firmly in the sand, they are disillusioned and disengaged from the day-to-day reality of the agency, hoping that things will somehow just happen on their own. But as Woody Allen said, "Eighty percent of success is just showing up." When it comes to execution, engaged leadership is paramount.

Look around the agency world and you'll see examples – past and present – of how engaged leadership created the most successful agencies.

Ogilvy & Mather	David Ogilvy
Doyle Dane Bernbach	Bill Bernbach
Chiat/Day	Jay Chiat

Wells Rich Green	Mary Wells
Fallon	Pat Fallon
Weiden & Kennedy	Dan Weiden
The Richards Group	Stan Richards

While there are plenty of differences in style and culture among these agencies, they all have one thing in common: a committed, passionate, and involved leader.

WITHOUT EXECUTION, THERE IS NO STRATEGY

A visionary military commander with brilliant strategies has no hope of winning a battle without equally brilliant tactics. Far too many leaders dismiss tactics as something for someone else to worry about. CEOs think of themselves as being above the fray of logistics. As Tom Peters observes, "It doesn't matter how brilliant your vision and strategy are if you can't get the soldiers, the weapons, the vehicles, the gasoline, the chow – the boots, for God's sake! – to the right people, at the right place, at the right time." Peters contends that the guy who won the first Gulf War wasn't Norman Schwartzkopf, but Gus Pagonis, "the genius who managed all of the logistics."[12]

Are tactics the same thing as execution? Most definitely not. Tactics are the specific steps required to fulfill a strategy, but execution is the discipline of getting tactics and strategies done. Execution is not an event – it's a practice in and of itself that an organization either does well or it doesn't. Execution is either a part of a company's culture or it's not.

Lest we dwell too much on philosophy and not enough on execution (which would tend to make this whole chapter irrelevant), let's look at some concrete ways to make performance happen in your organization.

ORGANIZING TEAMS TO MAKE IT HAPPEN

Each of the teams you assign to identify, prioritize, and carry out your initiatives in the areas of product, people, promotion, process and place need the following roles represented on the team:[13]

1. **Sponsor.** The agency partner or principal who gives official sanction to the initiatives and has the ability to authorize expenditures of agency time, money, or other resources.
2. **Leader.** The agency executive assigned to champion the initiatives for that particular team, drive the process, make assignments, and coordinate with other team leaders.
3. **Manager.** The person assigned to orchestrate the logistics, set the due dates, set the meetings, issue the status reports, and otherwise orchestrate the logistics of accomplishing the initiatives.

Unusual results require unusual effort.

4. **Owners.** The individual team members who are given primary responsibility for carrying out individual initiatives.
5. **Contributors.** The functional people in the agency who have the specific capabilities or knowledge needed to accomplish each of the initiatives.

Let's look at the team assigned to carry out "product" initiatives as an example. Let's say the *sponsor* is you, one of the agency principals. You select one of your department heads as the *leader* of the product team. The leader then chooses a *manager* to keep the team organized. The leader also selects an *owner* to head up each of the individual product initiatives. Each owner then selects individual *contributors* needed to execute the initiatives.

These complementary roles are vital to the success of the team. Properly organized, each team will have the responsibility, the capability, and the authority to make things happen. If your teams are lacking any of these roles, you'll be much less effective because:

- A team without a *sponsor* lacks the authority to spend the time and money.
- A team without a *leader* lacks the ability to make decisions and keep moving things forward.
- A team without a *manager* lacks the organization and discipline to keep commitments and meet deadlines.
- A team without *owners* for each individual initiative lacks the necessary focus on specific tasks.

- A team without *contributors* lacks the specialized capabilities and know-how to get things done.

What kind of people do you need on your team? Resist the temptation to select team leaders and members out of obligation or simply because they already hold positions of responsibility in the agency. What's needed is a team of *doers*. People who know how to execute, how to follow through, and how to get the job done. Use this as your primary selection criterion and you'll multiply your odds of success. Of course it's important to have the involvement, participation, and buy-in of your senior managers. Just make sure that you surround them with people who have the capacity, the drive, and the energy to get things done. These are the people in your organization who have already have a track record of accomplishment.

DECIDING WHAT NOT TO DO

Unless you enter a time warp when you step through your office door in the morning, tomorrow will be just as hectic as today. You simply can't work on agency initiatives "when you have the time," because you never will. There are always more things to do in a day than you have time for. You are always in a time deficit.

In order to give proper attention to important agency initiatives, the solution isn't deciding what to do. It's deciding what *not* to do. You must decide which things you will say "no" to, so you can say "yes" to the vital work of aligning your agency behind your brand. Unless you make deliberate decisions about how you spend your time, the waves of daily events will keep sweeping you out to sea.

Jim Collins studied the way 1,435 companies performed over a span of 40 years and came to a startling conclusion about why only 11 of them became great. It has nothing to do with smart acquisitions, charismatic CEOs, or motivating people with stock options. Instead, it is the result of a consistent, pragmatic process that keeps each company and its people on track for the long haul – what Collins calls "the victory of steadfast discipline." After five years of research, Collins published his findings in his landmark book *Good to Great*. His ultimate conclusion? If we just focus our attention on the right things – and stop doing the senseless things that consume so much time and energy – we can create powerful change without increasing the number of hours we work. Says Collins, "The real path to greatness, it turns out, requires simplicity and diligence. It requires clarity, not instant illumination. It demands each of us to focus on what is vital — and to eliminate all of the extraneous distractions."[14]

You can set the example for the rest of the organization. Begin each day by deciding which tasks are truly urgent, and which just have the appearance of being urgent. As soon as you complete the genuinely critical duties of the day, move immediately to the tasks that are important but not pressing. Consciously decide what you will do and not do. Refuse to devote time to something simply because it is presenting itself (such as a ringing phone or a voice mail message light).

When it comes to performance, the only wrong course of action is no action.

Devote work to your initiatives in the morning, when you're still fresh and have good energy. Resist the urge to get all the small stuff out of the way so you can work on the big stuff. Turn it around and work on the big stuff first, leaving the small stuff if you have time. Work on important tasks in large chunks of uninterrupted time — at least 60 to 90 minutes. For an hour and a half, ignore your inbox, pay no attention to phone calls, forget about e-mail, turn away visitors, and focus on the job at hand.

As the old Hoosier saying goes, "Knowing it ain't the same as doing it." The job of the executive is to execute.

BUILDING ACCOUNTABILITY

When it comes to working for clients, agencies are generally good at setting due dates, establishing timelines, and issuing conference reports. You should apply the same kind of discipline to effectively execute your internal initiatives. What's needed are mechanisms to make things happen. These performance mechanisms should include such things as:

1. Agency-wide meetings to discuss or announce agency direction or initiatives.
2. Regular meetings with individual teams to review the progress of specific initiatives.
3. Written reports showing the status of individual initiatives.

4. An intranet or extranet dedicated to the agency's purpose, principles, positioning, and practices, showing the initiatives the agency is working on and the teams assigned to accomplish them.

5. Frequent communication with the staff via e-mail or newsletters reviewing the goals of the agency in each practice area and the progress of major agency initiatives.

One of the most useful performance mechanisms is a written status report that answers the following questions:

- A written description of the *initiative* being addressed.
- Specific *tasks* required to complete the initiative.
- *Person responsible* for each of the specific tasks.
- *Date* the persons responsible are expected to accomplish their tasks.
- *Resources* required to complete each task, including staff time, money, technology, etc.
- *Target completion date* for finishing work on the initiative.

Let's say the team assigned to the area of "people" has a total of five initiatives. In addition to the team *leader* and *manager,* this team would also have five *owners* – one for each of the initiatives. The *owner* of each initiative is responsible for creating and updating a status report showing the individual tasks, assignments, and due dates required to accomplish their respective initiatives. The team *manager* is responsible for preparing and updating a master status report showing the progress of all initiatives on the people team.

Is this approach too left-brained for a right-brained enterprise? As everyone who has ever worked in an advertising agency knows, nothing gets done without a deadline. And unless you break a major project into small, individual tasks, it will forever loom as something too ambitious to tackle.

Organizations that execute have established performance as a discipline – a system for getting things done.

It's equally important to share the status of your initiatives with employees at large via staff meetings or e-mail briefings. Let everyone in the organization know that there isn't just a lot of talk about these initiatives – there's also a lot of action.

Finally, you must take responsibility to make sure your teams have everything they need to accomplish their objectives. Max DePree, the legendary leader of Herman Miller, believed that it's one thing to hold your people accountable, and quite another thing to give them the re-sources they need. "Leaders own assets," says DePree. They must deliver to their organizations the appropriate tools and equipment that people in the organization need to be accountable.[15]

OVERCOMING RESISTANCE

What are the possible reasons your initiatives could fail? Your list might include things like:

- Lack of commitment from senior management.
- Lack of buy-in from the staff.
- Lack of clear expectations, roles and responsibilities.
- Lack of time given current workloads and the pressure to be billable.

Now decide how you will meet this kind of resistance when it happens. Be prepared to meet these issues head on. Encourage discussion and debate. Create an environment in which questions and concerns can be openly addressed.

Very often, the main culprit threatening to sabotage your success is plain old indecisiveness. When difficult decisions about the direction of the agency are put on hold, your team feels immobilized – if not demoralized. Business books are littered with examples of companies who failed to move forward not because they couldn't, but because they couldn't *decide*. The only wrong course of action is *no* action.

GENERATING AND CELEBRATING SHORT TERM RESULTS

While many of the initiatives are long-term in nature, it's *essential* that each team is able to show some short-term results as well. For each major initiative, establish small interim goals that can be accomplished in a short amount of time, and reward and publicize the achievement of these goals. This gives the team – and the entire organization – the sense that something good is happening. One success can then build on another.

You can foster further gains by recognizing and rewarding the people who make these short-term wins possible. Acknowledge them in agency meetings and internal meetings. Celebrate their immediate successes, and you'll be giving them the emotional fuel they need to reach their long-term objectives.

The change you desire in your organization starts with you.

For example, you may have an initiative in the area of "Place" to completely renovate your office space to make it a better reflection of your agency brand. While a full overhaul of the offices may be what the agency needs, it's a pretty tall order. Better to break the initiative into do-able chunks, like starting with the reception area. When that's done, stop to recognize the people who did the work and the difference it has made to the agency, then move onto the next phase of the initiative.

Organizations that execute have established performance as a discipline – a system for getting things done. They also know that performance starts at the top, and that the behavior of the organization is determined by the behavior of its leaders. Darwin said, "It is not the strongest of the species that survive, nor the most intelligent, but the one most responsive to change." The change you desire in your organization starts with you.

THE OUTCOME OF BUILDING AN AGENCY BRAND

12 PROFIT: The End, But Not The Means

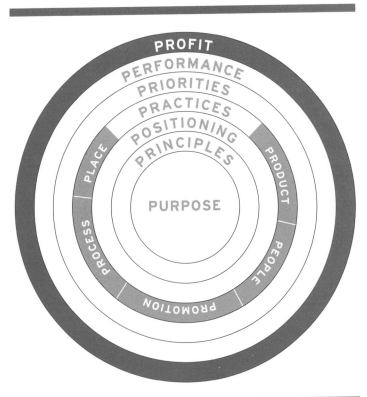

THE PARADOX OF the work you're doing with your agency is that if you have a strong purpose that transcends making money, you'll make money. That's why this is the shortest chapter in this book.

Your goal should be to run a focused, engaged business – not to earn a profit. The natural result, however, is that you will earn a profit. If you try and approach profitability from the other direction – from the outside in – you will resign yourself not only to a less successful business, but to a less meaningful existence. That's nothing to be taken lightly.

Viktor Frankl, the Austrian psychiatrist who survived the Nazi death camps, understood better than most the cause-and-effect nature of success: "For success, like happiness, cannot be pursued; it must *ensue*... as the unintended side-effect of one's personal dedication to a cause greater than oneself."[1] You achieve a profitable agency not by concentrating on profit, but by focusing on:

1. A **purpose** that gives meaning to your business life and goes beyond making money.
2. **Principles** that guide your important business decisions.
3. A **positioning** that clearly defines not only what you are, but what you are not.

> If you have a strong purpose that transcends making money, you'll make money.

4. **Practices** that are aligned with your positioning in all key areas of your business – **product**, **people**, **promotion**, **process**, and **place**.
5. Well-defined **priorities** or key initiatives designed to advance your practices and bring them into alignment with your positioning.
6. **Performance** that elevates talk into action and makes execution part of your culture.

Profit is the end. But it's by no means the means. The way to build a profitable agency brand is from the inside out.

FINAL WORD:
A Long-Term Framework For Leading The Agency

IF YOU WERE HIRING AN ARCHITECT, wouldn't you want to hire one with a well designed home? If agencies represent themselves as experts about brands, then agencies themselves should be models of strong brands. And if you want to transform your agency from "ad maker" to "brand consultant," what better place to start than with your own brand? If you can transform your own brand, you can do it for your clients. After all is said and done, that may be the real value in doing for yourself what you strive to do for your clients. As Gandhi said, "We must become the change we seek in the world."

The model discussed in this book for defining and aligning your brand can serve as an architecture for every aspect of managing and leading the agency. Consider that virtually everything an agency does falls into one of the following now-familiar areas:

- Product
- People
- Process
- Promotion
- Place

These practice areas can serve as a guide for:

1. Identifying and assigning partner roles and responsibilities
2. Developing job descriptions.
3. Defining initiatives (by department or for the agency as a whole)
4. Setting up agency teams
5. Analyzing the agency's strengths, weaknesses, opportunities and threats
6. Setting agency, departmental, and individual goals
7. Organizing and conducting agency meetings (staff meetings, department meetings, annual meetings, etc.)

8. Creating and maintaining an agency intranet
9. Organizing the agency filing system (computer network, etc.)
10. Filing agency library materials
11. Reporting agency news (newsletters, etc.)
12. Writing and organizing the employee handbook
13. Conducting new employee orientations
14. Organizing an agency training program

AN ARCHITECTURE FOR CLIENT BRANDING WORK

Rather than focusing exclusively on the area of *promotion,* agencies can become brand architects for their clients by *also* analyzing and addressing the areas of product, people, process, and place. Is this the domain of agencies? Typically, no. But if agencies want to move from "supplier" to "consultant," it will mean involvement in more aspects of the client's brand.

Consider how using all five dimensions of the brand – product, people, process, promotion, and place – can be used to deepen the agency's involvement with the client. These areas can serve as a way to develop and organize the tools the agency uses in serving its clients, including:

- Brand audits
- Recommendations
- Brand development plans
- Brand reviews
- Status reports

(Note the use of the language "brand audit" in place of "marketing audit" and "brand development plan" in place of "marketing plan." To fully represent the brand, agencies need to move beyond the domain of marketing to include the areas of operations, customer service, employee relations, etc.)

This, then, is the final frontier for marketing communications firms. Developing and managing the dimensions of your own brand so you can do the same for your clients. Between what today's clients really want (a strategy and creative vendor) and what they really *need* (a brand relationship firm) is the middle – where most agencies are now. And it's not a very desirable place to be. Marketing communications firms are at a point where they have an opportunity to make a quantum leap into a complete redefinition of their role in the business world. Doing the work of defining and aligning a brand in your own organization will help you learn how.

To thrive in the future, agencies will need to involve themselves at a much deeper level in their clients' business. The brand development model discussed in this book works just as well for clients as it does agencies. Is it practical for agencies to get involved with the *purpose* and *principles* of a company? Why not? Management consultants do. Some agencies consider it a crucial part of the value they bring to client relationships.

It goes without saying that *positioning* matters are the domain of agencies. Same for most aspects of *promotion.* But *product, people, process,* and *place* are in no man's land for the traditional marketing communications firm. How do you cross the chasm into these substantive areas of a client's brand? The same way you're doing it for your own organization. Start from the inside out. Help your clients assess their brand. Help them clarify the positioning for the brand. Then help them align all aspects of the brand behind that positioning. Moreover, if you help them identify their *priorities* or key brand initiatives, then serve as a catalyst to help them achieve *performance*, you'll become a much more valuable and relevant partner. That's where agencies are headed in the future. And your agency can be one of the first to get there.

APPENDIX:
Milestones of Success

How do you know if you've taken your agency through a successful positioning and alignment process? After six months or a year, stop and ask your management team the following questions:

PURPOSE

1. Are agency employees inspired by a sense of purpose that transcends making money?

PRINCIPLES

2. Does the agency have a well-understood set of values that guide important business decisions?

POSITIONING

3. Do we have a clear focus and positioning in the marketplace?

PRODUCT

4. Have we focused on what we do best and found strategic alliances for the rest?
5. Do we have proprietary approaches that add value to the agency brand?
6. Have we eliminated services that don't support the agency positioning?
7. Are we organized in a way that supports our differentiating business strategy?

PEOPLE

8. Do agency people have the right skill set to support the agency positioning?
9. Do we screen prospective employees for fit with the agency principles and positioning?
10. Do we orient new employees in agency purpose, principles, positioning, and practices?
11. Do we use performance reviews to help employees understand their contributions to the success of the agency brand?

12. Do we have an on-going professional development program that supports the goals of the agency brand?

PROMOTION

13. Do we have a clear set of criteria for identifying prospective clients?
14. Do our promotional materials reflect the agency brand (and avoid typical hyperbole)?
15. Have we developed a creative brief for the agency as a brand?
16. Do we have a good on-going self-promotion and publicity program to build the agency brand?

PROCESS

17. Do we have systems and procedures that support where agency is going instead of where it's been?
18. Are agency policies aligned our stated purpose, principles, and positioning?
19. Does our pricing and billing structure reflect our position in the marketplace?

PLACE

20. Do our offices reflect our desired brand identity?
21. Have we created a work environment that inspires productivity and supports the brand?
22. Do agency employees have the tools and resources they need to do their best work?

APPENDIX:
Assessing Your Agency Brand

Creating a successful agency brand means paying close attention to all the audiences that come in contact with the agency, including:

1. Employees
2. Prospective employees
3. Clients
4. Prospective clients
5. Agency search consultants
6. Business and trade press
7. Media sales representatives
8. Production partners
9. Industry leaders
10. Business and community leaders
11. Referral sources
12. Friends of the agency

To successfully manage the relationships between these audiences and your agency brand, you need good information. And the first place to start is with your own employees.

INTERNAL AGENCY BRAND ASSESSMENT

Conducting an internal assessment of your agency brand can give you deep insight into your employees' knowledge and attitudes regarding a wide range of topics — most importantly, how they perceive the focus and direction of the agency.

This assessment is completed by administering a questionnaire to all members of the agency staff. To make sure you're getting good information, all responses must be anonymous. It's best to find a credible outside source to administer the survey, since employees are more likely to give honest answers to a third party who promises to protect their identity. Answers should be ranked on a scale, ranging from "strongly disagree" to "strongly agree." Here are just a few examples of the kinds of questions an internal brand assessment should ask:

Product

- I believe the agency produces excellent creative work.
- I believe the agency has good strategic thinking skills.
- I believe the agency stays focused on what we do best instead of spreading ourselves too thin in areas where we don't have expertise.
- I believe the agency does a good job of integrating departments, services and capabilities to deliver a consistent marketing message for our clients.
- I believe the agency has good capabilities when it comes to understanding the consumer and discovering consumer insights.
- I believe agency management is committed to delivering a quality product.
- Etc. (Other questions should cover areas like proactivity, measuring results, being accountable to clients, etc.)

People

- I have a clear understanding of my role and what is expected of me.
- I feel agency management does a good job of keeping me informed of what's going on at the agency.
- I feel that new employees are given good training and orientation when they join the agency.
- I feel the agency has clear standards for the kind of people we hire.
- I feel the agency allows me the opportunity to grow and develop professionally.
- I feel the agency has an experienced and well-developed management team.
- I feel employees are fairly recognized and rewarded for the work they do.
- Etc. (Other areas of exploration ought to include opinions about the quality of the management team, the effectiveness of performance reviews, and whether or not employees feel vested in the success of the agency.)

Promotion

- I think the agency has an aggressive, well-organized new business program.
- I believe the agency is selective in the kind of new business we pursue.
- I think the agency has professional, up-to-date self-promotion materials.

- Etc. (This section should also ask such things as employees' views about the effectiveness of the agency's publicity program and to what extent management has developed specific criteria for prospective clients.)

Process

- I believe the agency has clear and well-understood systems and procedures.
- I believe we have an effective system for processing work through the agency.
- I believe agency teams work well together when developing strategic and creative recommendations.
- I feel the agency has a smooth well-run billing and accounting process.
- Etc. (Here you also have the opportunity to explore the effectiveness of the traffic system and which systems and procedures are actually counterproductive to the smooth operation of the agency.)

Place

- I feel the agency offices reflect well on the image of the company.
- I believe the agency provides a working environment in which everyone can do his or her best work.
- The agency supplies us with the necessary tools, resources and equipment to do our jobs.
- Etc. (This section should also explore issues like the physical layout of the offices and whether or not technology is used to its fullest advantage in the agency.)

When the results of the internal agency brand assessment are in, agency principals are always surprised to see the gaps between what they believe about the state of the agency and what the rank and file believes. For example, an agency founder who believed his agency was a model of integration was startled to learn that employees saw the agency as a disjointed collection of departments that rarely communicated. If integration of disciplines is an important dimension of your positioning, this kind of red flag will help you bring your organization into alignment.

You get the most value from this kind of information by sharing it with your entire staff – warts and all. This way, the whole team gets a picture of what needs to be done to align the agency's practices with its positioning. As the saying goes, the more you share, the more they care.

By completing an agency brand assessment, you establish a benchmark against which future success can be measured. You can then come back a year later – after you have worked on defining and aligning the agency brand – and field the assessment again. If you have taken your branding work seriously, you'll be pleased to see marked improvements in many (if not most) areas. It's important to share these results with your employees as well. The entire agency will be motivated and encouraged by the difference between the "before" and the "after." The agency brand assessment can then become an annual event – a tool to help you monitor success, measure employee satisfaction, and fine-tune the way you lead and manage the agency.

EXTERNAL AGENCY BRAND ASSESSMENT

An external version of this assessment can help evaluate how the agency brand is performing from the point of view of your clients. This is a written questionnaire that employs both a rating system and open-ended questions in the following areas:

Client Questions

1. Knowledge of clients business
2. Giving strategic input and marketing counsel
3. Experience and depth of the account team
4. Staying in regular contact
5. Anticipating needs without waiting to be asked
6. Listening to and understanding client concerns
7. Executing agreed-upon strategies
8. Keeping within budgets
9. Meeting deadlines
10. Taking responsibility for mistakes
11. Quality of work
12. Enthusiasm and commitment of agency
13. Ease of doing business with the agency
14. Producing desired results

Beyond clients, other audiences also have an influence on the success of your agency brand, including:

- Agency search consultants
- Trade press editors and reporters
- Business press editors and reporters
- Industry association leaders
- Media reps

These audiences can be asked questions like the following:

1. How would you describe (<u>agency name</u>) to someone who doesn't know them?
2. What would you say (<u>agency name</u>) is most known for?
3. What kind of experience do you generally have when you come in contact with (<u>agency name</u>)?
4. If you could offer any feedback or advice as to how (<u>agency name</u>) could improve their operation or relationships, what would it be?

Armed with results from both internal and external sources, you'll have the critical information you need to initiate and track changes to your organization.

REVELATIONS FROM AN AGENCY BRAND ASSESSMENT

The findings from an Agency Brand Assessment are not only food for thought for agency management; they point the way to areas the agency must address to achieve its branding strategy. Here's how a well-respected agency summarized some of the findings from their agency brand assessment:

Account Management. "While account managers appear to be in control of their respective accounts, there is a perception that account management is a weak link in the agency. This feeling is fueled by the perception that none of the partners are as involved in client relationships and strategic leadership as they could or should be. The partners are seen as bright and capable, but agency staffers believe that they are not taking the initiative to actively contribute to addressing client issues and problems."

Creative. "There is a clear feeling that the creative work at the agency is the best it's ever been, and that the agency has elevated its creative standards under new creative leadership. What was once a perceived weakness of the agency (or at least a neutral factor) is now seen as a competitive strength."

Teamwork and Integration. "Agency morale is almost universally described as 'the worst it's ever been,' owing to several factors described in the assessment. At the top of the list is the 'lack of communication between the partners.' Contributing to the problem is a perceived change in management style that has transformed the culture from one of benevolence and self-governance to one of rules and regulations.

Staffing. "Many feel that the agency has not hired wisely, and that there are several ineffective members of the agency team. They are critical of the fact that agency management has not acted to address the "bad apples" problem. There is also a feeling that the agency is not committed to developing, growing and advancing its own people, and that management is more likely to look on the outside for new talent than to give a new opportunity to someone already on staff. This is associated with a perceived lack of training and mentoring at the agency."

New Business. "The staff expresses genuine concern about the lack of new business success at the agency. There is an interest and willingness on the part of the staff to help out in new business, but they feel they are not informed or kept up to date on new business activities. Furthermore, they see the new business effort as 'spearfishing' instead of focusing on accounts that are right for the agency."

Agency Focus. "Related to the issue of new business is the feeling that the agency lacks a focus and has failed to brand and promote itself effectively to the client community. Self-promotion efforts in general are seen as languishing."

Needless to say, this agency had some work to do. For the partners, the agency brand assessment opened their eyes to some blind spots. To their credit, this agency worked hard to develop a positioning and worked to bring their important practices into line.

APPENDIX:
Keeping More Of What You've Got

You've built a flourishing agency brand and earned earn healthy fees for your work. Of course, just because you've generated good income doesn't necessarily mean you've turned in good profits. Even some unprofitable firms bring in a fair amount of income. They just need to *keep more of it.*

Even with a well-developed purpose and positioning, you still have to proactively manage the bottom line. Many agencies turn in unprofitable quarters and unprofitable years not because they didn't make the money, but because don't have the information they need to understand where their money is going.

The nature of profitability is interdependence. You can't have a profitable agency if you don't have profitable clients. You can't have profitable clients if you don't earn a profit on individual jobs or assignments. And you can't earn a profit on assignments if your employees aren't productive and billable. When it comes to managing the margin, you have to pay attention to each of these areas — not just the bottom line.

EMPLOYEE PROFITABILITY

At the most basic level, profitability starts with people who are able to charge for the value of their time. Most agency managers are focused on the question of being overstaffed or understaffed, but the more essential issue is the productivity of the people you already have.

In laws firms, billable time is sacred. Most attorneys are expected to turn in time sheets with at least 80% of their time charged to client business. Now that most agencies earn their income the same way as law firms — based on the value of their time — it's essential to have clear standards about billable time.

So what do agencies that excel in employee productivity and profitability have in common?

They Have a Good System for Reporting Time

As elementary as it may seem, profitability starts with making sure *every* employee – including the principals – completes a daily timesheet. More importantly, make sure all timesheets are actually turned in. Policing timesheets is a fine art, which the most profit-minded agencies take very seriously.

Simply accounting for 8 hours a day isn't enough. Agencies lose a tremendous amount of billable time that doesn't get logged on timesheets because the time was spent at home in the evening or on weekends. Log all your client-related time, whether it was spent in the office or not. And consider what to do with the question of billing for travel time. Paying salaries to people who travel a lot on client business and then not collecting income for it creates a profitability challenge.

Finally, take pains to minimize time logged as "non-billable" client time. "Non-billable" client time should be logged only in two instances: Ramp-up time spent at the beginning of a client relationship, or time spent correcting agency errors.

They Have Billable Time Goals

The best agencies strive for 80% billable time. For rank and file billable staff members, this is actually quite realistic. Managers who spend time on agency business will have lower billable time goals, perhaps 70% or sometimes even 60%. The important thing is to have a billable time goal for each employee, each department, and the agency as a whole. Then make sure you measure and report it on a monthly basis. What gets measured gets managed.

They Keep Their Staffing Levels in Check

It's a fact that agencies are happier and more effective when they're run in a slightly understaffed mode. It's far better to have fewer really good, well-paid people than a lot of people with average abilities. In no case should your salary cost exceed 50% of your gross income. Another good measure of staffing levels is to generate at least $125,000 in gross income per employee (the most productive agencies earn far more than that).

And of course none of these ratios will be of much use if you are undercharging for the value of your time. It's amazing how many firms keep increasing salaries without increasing their hourly rates. Set your hourly rates based on the employee's base hourly compensation times three, and don't hesitate to inform your clients that your hourly rates are subject to change on an annual basis. A blended hourly rate for the agency as a whole is just as good or better.

JOB PROFITABILITY

The least-measured element in the chain of agency profitability is the individual job or assignment. That's somewhat understandable, given that most agencies have hundreds if not thousands of open jobs at any given moment. The point isn't to evaluate the profitability of every single job that goes through the system. All you need is a spot check of each account on a periodic basis.

How do profitable agencies make sure their assignments are profitable?

They Continually Improve Their Estimates

In evaluating the profitability of individual jobs, you can look at two different aspects. First, how close did you come to the original estimate? Second, did you make a fair profit on the job?

A lot of agencies have an eye-opening experience when they take the time to compare job estimates against actuals. It suddenly explains why an account – or even the whole agency – has been losing money. They find that they have been systematically underestimating the number of agency hours required to complete their assignments, probably by at least 10%. Making this assessment, then sharing the information with management and staff, can have a dramatic effect on earnings.

They Charge for Client Changes

The main killer on job profitability is, of course, client revisions. Do you build sufficient time in your estimates for the inevitable changes from the client? Or do you charge additional agency hours for client revisions? If you do neither of these things, you're setting yourself up for unprofitable assignments.

They Control Cancelled Time

The hidden profit eradicator on assignments is agency time that is cancelled or written off. It's remarkable how many agencies fail to capture and assess the amount of time that is written off each month by its account managers. Even in small agencies, cancelled time can often amount to hundreds of thousands of dollars – dollars that would otherwise go straight to the bottom line. Measure cancelled time and you'll see where a lot of your profitability problems have been hiding.

CLIENT PROFITABILITY

An analysis of client profitability often reveals a picture in which only half the agency's clients are profitable. This creates a situation in which the unprofitable clients ride on the coattails of the profitable ones. Serious agency financial managers insist that each client pay its way. What's the point of keeping a client that actually costs you money?

The most obvious way to solve client profitability problems is to adjust staffing or service levels – fewer people or fewer hours going against the business. But first check to see if you have other issues lurking beneath the surface. Are you underestimating individual assignments and incurring excessive write-offs? Are you spending agency time for which you are not being adequately compensated through commissions or fees – particularly in the areas of account management or account planning? Are you recovering excessive out-of-pocket charges associated with this client?

After completing your diagnosis, you may come to the conclusion that the account is being run efficiently, but there simply isn't enough income from the client to pay for the work required. It's then that you must have a discussion with the client about either reducing the work or increasing the income. Reducing the time you spend on the business without also reducing the workload or client expectations might lead to short-term profitability, but it's sure to lead to long-term frustration on the part of the client.

How do financially successful agencies address client profitability?

They Take an Open Book Approach With Clients

Ultimately, an open-book financial policy with clients is the way to address and solve profitability problems. Keep good cost-accounting records and share them with clients when needed. Show them the exact income and expenses on their business. Reasonable clients expect their agencies to earn a reasonable profit, and if you can show that their business is being run efficiently, most will agree to adjustments that allow you to earn money. Being up front with clients about money gives you a forum to discuss profitability problems. On the other hand, if you view client compensation with a "black box" mentality, afraid to disclose financial matters for fear of losing the account, your fears may be realized.

They Recover the Value of All Agency Time

Sometimes agencies forget that to be profitable, they must at least recover the value of each hour spent on behalf of a client. When agency partners spend time on a client's business, yet neglect to record the time or turn in a timesheet, they are literally giving away their product. When hoards of agency people attend client meetings without billing for it, the client might be pleased but the agency bottom line takes a direct hit. One way or another, commissions or fees, markups or hourly rates, agencies must be paid fair value for each hour they spend on a client's business. If you want to "give away" such things as partner time, you'd better raise the rates you charge on everything else. It's an illusion to think otherwise.

AGENCY PROFITABILITY

The easiest way to increase overall agency profitability is to increase income, and the easiest way to increase income is from current clients. The senior person responsible for each client should have a proactive plan for growing current client business using new ideas or services that could genuinely benefit the client.

Income from new clients is a more difficult proposition, but can lead to even faster results on the bottom line, because expenses tend to fall six months or so behind new income (hiring additional staff, etc.).

Beyond the obvious solution of adding more income, here's how the best agencies address some overlooked areas that can siphon agency profits.

They Recoup Their Expenses

Many agencies give away what other professional service firms are very careful to charge for. In today's world of razor-thin margins, having a good system for charging for miscellaneous expenses can mean the difference between a small profit and no profit at all. And it goes beyond just billing back travel and overnight deliveries.

Most agency compensation agreements state that the agency has the right to bill back all out-of-pocket expenses associated with the client's business. While a lot of agencies think to include long-distance telephone and color copies, they often overlook such things as cell phones – a significant client-related expense. Part of the reason is because it is such a hassle to count every photocopy, record every fax, code every phone call, etc. Some agency managers reach the conclusion that it's just not worth the trouble. That's the wrong conclusion.

Just simplify the process. First of all, billing back travel expenses, overnight delivery, etc. is easy because it's easy to assign a job number to these items. Billing for phone, fax, copies, etc. is the problem. The solution is to bill for these expenses on a pro-rated basis. Take all the client-related miscellaneous expenses for the month and charge them back to clients based on the percent of income each individual client generated that month. If a particular client generated 12% of that's month's income, they are allocated 12% of that month's total client-related miscellaneous expenses.

They Recover Their Investment in Technology

What printer would buy a new press and not build the cost into his pricing structure? Agencies buy specialized technology and equipment routinely without giving a second thought to how to make it pay out. That's because despite the technology revolution, agencies are still in the mindset of selling time, not goods and services produced by equipment.

Unless you have found a way to recoup your considerable annual investment in technology, you are literally giving away services that directly benefit your clients. Of course basic desktop PCs can fairly be consider part of agency overhead, but what about the specialized hardware and software in the creative and production departments? Agencies lay out hundreds of thousands of dollars to purchase not only computers capable of high-end graphics, but pricey color printers, highly specialized graphics software, fonts, images, stock libraries, ad infinitum. Keep in mind that these are all things that clients would have to purchase for themselves – particularly photo discs and type fonts – yet agencies simply try to absorb these expenses as part of the cost of doing business.

The litmus test is this: if your clients would have to buy and maintain this specialized hardware and software themselves if they produced their own work, it's fair and reasonable for the agency to charge clients for it. The question is how? Again, keep it simple. Most agencies have found that on average, the costs of buying and maintaining the specialized technology and resources they need amounts to about 2% of the cost of each job. In other words, if a print ad costs $20,000 to produce, the specialized "digital imaging" expenses associated with that job would be 2%, or $400. By itself, that isn't a lot of money, but multiply it by the number of assignments you complete each year and suddenly you've made back what you invested in technology that directly benefits your clients.

They Manage Their Cash

Finally, it's one thing to earn a profit on paper and another thing to actually have the money in hand. At the end of the day, cash management is the real lifeblood of the agency.

Good cash management starts with timely billing. The most diligent agencies issue billing within 10 days of closing the monthly billing cycle. On the other end, they are conscientious about collections, making sure receivables over 60 days account for no more than 5% of average monthly billing.

Another cornerstone of superior cash management is to estimate and bill as many charges in advance as possible, both production and media. Look at it this way. By the time the agency incurs an expense from an outside supplier, gets it into the agency billing cycle, issues an invoice to the client, and gives the client 30 days to pay, the agency has likely already paid the vendor invoice. This makes the agency a bank for the client – not exactly what you're in business for. By estimating jobs in advance and issuing a bill to the client at the beginning of the job – not the end – the agency receives payment from the client in time to pay its suppliers.

This is even more important when it comes to media placement. Given the huge sums of money involved in media, the drain on agency cash flow can be considerable. Agencies should estimate all media costs 60 days in advance, then bill and collect from clients in time to make payments to the media.

They Measure So They Can Manage

It's quite remarkable to see agency managers grouse about agency finances and profitability while leaving their people almost completely in the dark on the subject. In agencies like these, financials are tightly-guarded secrets for the eyes of owners only; beyond the income statement and balance sheet, key measures of agency financial performance aren't reported or analyzed, much less shared with those in a position to do something about it.

Contrast this with the open-book approach of progressive agency managers, who share virtually everything except confidential salary and bonus information. They involve their senior managers deeply in the financial management of the agency. And they have an arsenal of reports to help them monitor and diagnose the financial health of the agency (see "The Agency Financial Meeting" at the end of this chapter).

By providing senior managers with monthly profitability reports (by employee, by department, and by client) they can get to the heart of profitability problems and take appropriate action. The same goes for policing write-offs and past due accounts. If you give your key people the financial tools they need, you truly can make them responsible for the financial health of their people and their clients. Otherwise, you'll have to settle for the idea of the partners reviewing secret reports in secret meetings and continue to wonder why nobody cares that the agency isn't making money.

Beyond senior managers, every employee of the agency should feel some ownership and involvement in the financial health of the agency. For starters, teach your people how the agency makes money (you'd be surprised how many of them don't really understand this). Then share with the entire staff the main indicators of financial success in the form of a monthly "key numbers" report (see "The Agency Financial Scorecard" at the end of the chapter).

They Share the Wealth

The ultimate way to have your people feel vested in the financial success of the agency is to *make* them vested by sharing the agency's profits. An agency-wide profit sharing program also allows you to keep salaries at a reasonable level, while at the same time providing a financial incentive to employees.

There are countless methods for devising profit sharing programs, ranging from a completely arbitrary system that rewards only selected individuals to one that is highly methodical that rewards literally everybody in the company. The system you choose and use will have a lot to do with the personality and culture of the agency, but the important point is to *have* a system, and make sure everyone understands what it is and how it works. It's an axiom of business that the way to create wealth is to share wealth.

▬▬▬

Jim Mullen ran Mullen with the philosophy that a great agency must be both an artistic success and a commercial success. "In many ways," says Mullen, "leadership in profitability is as much a measure of corporate greatness as the most esteemed honor by the most revered industry authority."[1]

THE AGENCY FINANCIAL SCORECARD

These critical measures of financial success should be tracked and reported monthly.

	YTD Actual	YTD Goal	Variance	Annual Goal
Gross Income				
Staffing Expense				
Staffing Expense % of GI				
Total Operating Expenses				
Total operating Expenses % of GI				
Operating Profit				
Operating Profit % of GI				

% Direct Time – Agency Average
% Direct time – By Department

	Current Month	YTD	Goal
Gross Income per Employee			

	Current Month	YTD	Annual Limit
Cancelled Charges - Time			
Cancelled Charges – Outside Expenses			

	30 Days	60 Days	90 Days	120 Days
Accounts Receivable				

	Gross Income	Operating Profit	% of Gross Income
Client Profitability – Agency Average			
Client Profitability – By Client			

	Current Month	Goal
Cash		

	Current Month
Work in Progress - Time	
Work in Progress - Outside Expenses	

NOTES:

CHAPTER 1

1 Bill Bernbach, *Bill Bernbach Said,* DDB Worldwide Communications Group, 2002.
2 Allen Rosenshine, "Without Great Work, Then Nothing Else Really Matters," *Advertising Age,* July 26, 1999.
3 Adam Morgan, *Eating the Big Fish*, John Wiley & Sons, 1999.
4 Shaun McIlrath, "A New Creative Revolution," *Admap*, September 2002.
5 Jack Trout, *Differentiate or Die*, John Wiley & Sons, 2002.
6 Michael Treacy and Fred Wiersema, The Discipline of Market Leaders, HarperCollins, 1995.
7 James X. Mullen, *The Simple Art of Greatness*, Viking, 1995.
8 Kenneth Roman and Jane Mass, *How to Advertise,* St. Martin's Press, 1976.
9 Al Ries, *Focus*, HarperBusiness, 1996.
10 Jack Trout, *Differentiate or Die*, John Wiley & Sons, 2002.

CHAPTER 2

1 Joey Reiman, *Thinking for a Living*, Longstreet, 1998.
2 Jeremy Bullmore, "Was There Life before Mission Statements?" *Marketing Magazine*, July 10, 1997.
3 James C. Collins and Jerry I. Porras, "Building Your Company's Vision," *Harvard Business Review*, September-October 1996.
4 Peter Drucker, *The Effective Executive*, HarperBusiness, 1996.
5 Gary Hamel, *Leading the Revolution,* Harvard Business School Press, 2000.
6 Warren Bennis and Patricia Ward Beiderman, *Organizing Genius*, Addison-Wesley Publishing Co., 1997.
7 Daniel Goleman, Richard Boyatzis, and Annie McKee, *Primal Leadership*, Harvard Business School Press, 2002.
8 Thomas J. Peters and Robert H. Waterman, Jr., *In Search of Excellence,* Harper & Row, 1982.
9 W. Edwards Deming, *Out of the Crisis,* MIT Press, 2000.
10 Jean-Marie Dru, *Disruption,* John Wiley & Sons, 1996.
11 Robert B. Reich, "The Company of the Future," *Fast Company,* November 1998.

12 Gay Hendricks and Kate Ludeman, *The Corporate Mystic*, Bantam Books, 1996.

13 James C. Collins and Jerry I. Porras, "Building Your Company's Vision," *Harvard Business Review*, September-October 1996.

CHAPTER 3

1   John Robertson and John Vitro, VitroRobertson, *Agency Capabilities*, 1999.

2   James C. Collins and Jerry I. Porras, "Building Your Company's Vision," *Harvard Business Review*, September-October 1996.

3   John Robertson and John Vitro, VitroRobertson, *Agency Capabilities*, 1999.

4   Tom Nelson and Steve Gardner, "Dèja Vu Vu Vu," *Adweek*, September 18, 2000, p. 16.

5   Tim Williams and Scott Rockwood, Williams & Rockwood, *Manifesto*, 1994.

6   Stephen R. Covey, *Principle-Centered Leadership*, Summit Books, 1990.

7   "Transformation by Design: An Interview with Dee Hock," *What is Enlightenment?*, Fall/Winter 2002.

8   David Ogilvy, *Principles of Management*, Ogilvy & Mather, 1968.

9   David Ogilvy, *Principles of Management*, Ogilvy & Mather, 1968.

10 Dave Newbold, *The Agency Bible,* 1995.

11 From a speech by Dan Wieden as quoted in "Why Size Doesn't Matter," *One: A Magazine*, Volume 6, Issue 2.

12 Warren Berger, "Carmichael Lynch," *Communication Arts,* September/October 1996.

13 Martin Puris, *Adweek Agency Directory,* 1988/89.

14 Richard Kirshenbaum and Jonathan Bond, *Under the Radar*, John Wiley & Sons, 1998.

15 Jim Collins, "How Walmart Got Great," *Fast Company,* June 2003.

16 Marcus Buckingham and Donald O. Clifton, *Now, Discover Your Strengths*, The Free Press, 2001.

17 Jim Osterman, "Home Is Where The Art Is," *Adweek,* May 24, 1999.

18 *The Marsteller Method*, Marsteller Inc., New York, p. 104.

19 Stanley Pollitt, "How I Started Account Planning In Agencies," *Campaign*, April 20, 1979.

20 Charles Decker, *99 Principles and Practices of Procter & Gamble's Success*, Pocket Books, 1998.

CHAPTER 4

1 Warren Berger, "Riddell Advertising & Design," *Communication Arts,* September/October 1995.
2 Al Ries, *Focus*, HarperBusiness, 1996.
3 Tom Rosensteel, "Project for Excellence in Journalism," as reported on National Public Radio.
4 "Your Next Move," *Fast Company*, July 2003.
5 Theodore Leavitt, *Thinking About Management*, 1991.
6 Selected chapter titles from *Differentiate or Die* by Jack Trout, John Wiley & Sons, 2000.
7 Michael Marsak of Effective Marketing Strategies, Surprise, Arizona.
8 Edwin R. French, *French & Partners, Inc.: What We Are All About,* 1988.
9 Austin Howe, "The Power of Four," Four Stories press release November 18, 2002.
10 Tom Chappell, *Managing Upside Down,* William Morrow & Company, 1999.
11 Luke Sullivan, *Hey Whipple, Squeeze This,* John Wiley & Sons, 1998.
12 Sun Tzu, *The Art of War*, Delacorte Press, 1983.

INTRODUCTION TO SECTION 3

1 Stan Richards, *The Peaceable Kingdom*, John Wiley & Sons, 2001.
2 Daniel Goleman, Richard Boyatzis, and Annie McKee, *Primal Leadership*, Harvard Business School Press, 2002.

CHAPTER 5

1 Jonathan Bond and Richard Kirshenbaum, *Under The Radar,* John Wiley & Sons, 1998.
2 Tom Monahan, "Broken Funny Bones and Frayed Heart Strings," *Communication Arts*, Photography Annual 1998.
3 John Hegarty, *Adweek*, February 14, 1994.
4 Lee Clow, TBWA/Chiat/Day, APG-U.S. Conference, Santa Monica, California, August 1996.
5 Interview with Gary Goldsmith, "Can a Big Agency Think Small," *One: A Magazine*, Volume 6, Issue 2
6 *How to Swarm*, R&R Partners, 2000.

7   David Ogilvy, "50th Anniversary Luncheon Speech," Advertising Research Foundation, New York, March 1986.

8   Tom Monahan, *The Do-It-Yourself Lobotomy,* John Wiley & Sons, 2002.

9   Jonathan Bond and Richard Kirshenbaum, *Under The Radar,* John Wiley & Sons, 1998.

10 Stephen R. Covey, *The 7 Habits of Highly Successful People*, Simon & Schuster, 1989, p. 239.

11 Bill Bernbach, *Bill Bernbach Said,* DDB Worldwide Communications Group, 2002.

12 John Webster, APG-U.S. conference presentation, Miami, Florida, June 2000.

13 Jean-Marie Dru, *Disruption*, John Wiley & Sons, 1996.

14 Ram Charan, *What the CEO Wants You to Know*, Crown Business, 2001, p. 20.

15 Tom Duncan and Sandra Moriarty, *Driving Brand Value*, McGraw-Hill, 1997.

16 Dave Boede, *AdNews,* February 2003.

CHAPTER 6

1   Rob White, APG/US conference presentation, Miami, Florida, July 2000.

2   Scott Bedbury, *A New Brand World*, Viking Press, 2002.

3   Lamille Report, Top Executives of the 1990s.

4   Warren Bennis and Patricia Ward Beiderman, *Organizing Genius*, Addison-Wesley Publishing Co., 1997.

5   Peter Drucker, *The Effective Executive*, Harperbusiness, 1997.

6   Marcus Buckingham and Donald O. Clifton, *Now, Discover Your Strengths*, The Free Press, 2001.

7   David Ogilvy, *The Unpublished David Ogilvy,* The Ogilvy Group, 1986.

8   Warren Bennis and Patricia Ward Beiderman, *Organizing Genius*, Addison-Wesley Publishing Co., 1997.

9   James X. Mullen, *The Simple Art of Greatness,* Viking, 1995.

10 Stephen R. Covey, *The 7 Habits of Highly Successful People*, Simon & Schuster, 1989.

11 Agency of the Year 1998, *Adweek*, January 25, 1999.

12 Jack Stack, *The Great Game of Business*, Currency Doubleday, 1992.

13 Stan Richards, *The Peaceable Kingdom*, John Wiley & Sons, 2001.

CHAPTER 7

1   Jack Trout, *Differentiate or Die*, John Wiley & Sons, 2002

2   Bob Lundin, Jones Lundin Beals, as quoted in an article published by The List.

3   Ford Harding, *Rain Making,* Bob Adams, Inc., 1994

4   Jon Steel, *Truth, Lies & Advertising,* John Wiley & Sons, 1998.

5   Joe Klien, "How to Build a Better Democrat," *Time*, May 19, 2003.

6   Stuart Elliott, "Virgin Atlantic Cuts Short Review," *New York Times,* May 7, 2003.

7   Martin Puris, *AdWeek Agency Directory*, 1990.

8   David H. Maister, *True Professionalism*, The Free Press, 1997.

CHAPTER 8

1   Peter Drucker, *The Effective Executive*, HarperBusiness, 1996.

2   Peter Keen, *The Process Edge*, Harvard Business School Press, 1997,

CHAPTER 9

1   Lee Clow, "Creating An Inspirational Environment," *One: A Magazine,* Spring 2001.

2   David Ogilvy, *Principles of Management*, Ogilvy & Mather, 1968.

CHAPTER 10

1   As told in *The Corporate Mystic*, by Gay Hendricks and Kate Ludeman, Bantam Books, 1996.

2   Stephen R. Covey, *First Things First*, Simon & Schuster, 1994.

3   Larry Bossidy and Ram Charan, *Execution*, Crown Business, 2002.

4   Peter Drucker, *The Effective Executive*, HarperBusiness, 1996

CHAPTER 11

1   James C. Collins and Jerry I. Porras, "Building Your Company's Vision," *Harvard Business Review*, September-October 1996.

2   Adam Morgan, *Eating the Big Fish*, John Wiley & Sons, 1999.

3   David Maister, *True Professionalism*, The Free Press, 1997.

4   Jeffrey Pfeffer, interviewed by Alan M. Webber in *Fast Company,* June 2000.

5   J. Sterling Livingston, "Pygmalion in Management," *Harvard Business Review,* January 2003.

6   Peter Drucker, *The Practice of Management*, HarperBusiness, 1954.

7   Bill Bernbach, *Bill Bernbach Said,* DDB Worldwide Communications Group, 2002.

8   Paul Feldwick, "Building Brand Muscle," *Admap,* July/August 2002.

9   Daniel Goleman, Richard Boyatzis, and Annie McKee, *Primal Leadership*, Harvard Business School Press, 2002.

10 Max DePree, *Leadership is an Art,* Dell Publishing, 1989.

11 Larry Bossidy and Ram Charan, *Execution*, Crown Business, 2002.

12 Tom Peters, "Rule #3: Leadership is Confusing as Hell," *Fast Company,* March 2001.

13 Inspired by the model developed by Barclays Global Investors.

14 Jim Collins, "Good to Great," *Fast Company,* October 2001.

15 Max DePree, *Leadership is an Art,* Dell Publishing, 1989.

CHAPTER 12

1   Viktor Frankl, *Man's Search for Meaning,* Washington Square Press, 1997.

APPENDIX

1   James X. Mullen, *The Simple Art of Greatness*, Viking, 1995.

Acknowledgements

This book would never have happened without the constant support and encouragement of my wife, Christine, my constant companion for almost three decades. My daughter and professional associate, Emily Hicks, has been behind me every step of the way and did all of the behind-the-scenes work that helped make the book a reality. And my son, Desmond, who has flirted with the agency business, uses his philosophy degree to challenge how I see the world.

Over the years, I have learned tremendously from people I've worked with, including my former partner Scott Rockwood. I've benefited from advice from people like Stephen Covey and Tom Monahan. I deeply appreciate the support of my consulting clients, whose agencies served as catalysts for much of my thinking on the subject of agency management.

I'm indebted to my friend in the agency business Steve Cuno, who gave generous amounts of time reading, reviewing, and editing my manuscript. My librarian sister, Janet Williams, devoted countless hours to proofreading several versions of the manuscript and improved not only the "letter" but the "spirit" of the book as well.

Randall Smith and Bryan Wilson at design firm Modern 8 are architects of the cover concept and book design, while Pat Aylward at The Copy Workshop brought it all to life on the printed page. I also greatly appreciate the help of Bruce and Lorelei Bendinger at The Copy Workshop, who gave me the counsel and advice I needed to get through the process of publishing my first book.

Finally, I'm indebted to my original mentor, Ted French, for having the courage to give me my first job in advertising at Marsteller in New York. Ted is one of those rare people who has maintained his enthusiasm for the business throughout his life, and has encouraged me at important times all throughout my career.

About the Author

Tim Williams is founder and president of Ignition Consulting Group, a management consultancy devoted to helping marketing communications firms do for themselves what they do for their clients – build a great brand. With almost three decades of agency experience – including leading and managing several respected firms – Tim works as a consultant to marketing communications firms throughout the United States and abroad.

Before forming Ignition, Tim was president of nationally-ranked R&R Partners (creators of the "What happens here, stays here" campaign for Las Vegas) and was also co-founder of his own firm, Williams & Rockwood, now known as Richter 7. He spent his early career in New York and Houston working at agencies including Ogilvy & Mather and Marsteller, and has led efforts for a variety of well-known brands such as Compaq, NBC, American Express, IBM, National Public Radio, Hummer, and Novell.

Tim has been a speaker and workshop leader for associations, agency networks, universities, and business conferences sponsored by such organization as the American Association of Advertising Agencies, CBS Television, National Public Radio, the U.S. Small Business Administration, and The One Club.

During his career as an agency CEO and consultant, Tim has been featured and quoted in the *Wall Street Journal, New York Times, Advertising Age, Adweek, Brandweek, Marketing News, Print, and Creativity.* He has been a contributor to publications like *Communication Arts, The Advertiser, Marketing News, Admap,* and served as a regular columnist for *Ad Age Insider.*

The agencies under Tim's leadership have earned recognition in top national and international competitions including the Communications Arts Advertising and Design Annuals, The One Show, the Clio Awards, the Cannes Film Festival, and the National Addy's.

When he's not on the road speaking and consulting, Tim makes his home in the mountains of Utah, where he resides with his wife and two dogs.

More information about Ignition Consulting Group is available at www.ignitiongroup.com.